# Married To Mr Nasty

by

## Dr Annie Kaszina Ph.D.

# Copyright

*You will heal…*

*But he will always be a Narsehole*

# Contents

4

This Book That Will Tell You:


Why Your Partner Is Making You

MISERABLE,

Why Your Relationship Is NOT Working

*(And Never Will)*

And What YOU Need To Do

To Get Your Life Back On Track

# Foreword

The fact that you are reading this now means that you, or someone dear to you, is or has been in a relationship with *"Mr Nasty."*

Now, no woman ever willingly *"signs up"* for Mr Nasty. No woman consciously says to herself, *"I know. I'll take up with this man who clearly hates all women and will, before long, hate me also. I'll sign up cheerfully for years of disrespect, blame, abuse, criticism, and humiliation. I'll embrace feeling terrible about myself, being isolated from friends and family, and being treated like dirt. I look forward to spending my time walking on eggshells, and living in constant fear of another verbal attack, and/or another beating."*

**We are not crazy.**

Maybe we don't have a very clear idea about how to be happy, because happiness and healthy, supportive love were in short supply in the home in which we grew up.

Maybe, because we grew up in a home where love was in short supply, we believe that we have to give oodles and oodles of love before we deserve to be loved in return.

We certainly believe that frogs turn into princes. And I wonder how much we believe that because we see ourselves as Cinderella. Certainly a lot of women believe it will be sackcloth and ashes for them forever after, unless their prince comes along to save them.

For *"Cinderella women,"* Mr Nasty doesn't exist.

He simply does not feature in the fantasy map of relationships that they carry inside their own heart.

If he says he loves them, if he makes the right noises and shows signs of *"ticking some of their boxes,"* they naively assume that he is The One. At the very least, they believe he can be molded into The One.

They believe that they have got a Prince.

They overlook all the stuff that doesn't fit with their dreams and their aspirations.

Unfortunately, Mr Nasty does not run the same fantasy in his head that a Cinderella woman does.

Cinderella women find out, to their cost, that Mr Nasty sees himself as a kind of male Cinderella with a twist. He tells a really good story of having had a really rough time growing up. He may—or may not—have had a *"wonderful mother,"* but other women in his life have treated him very, very badly. As he tells it, he has a lot to be very angry about. And he is angry. With the benefits of hindsight, Cinderella women come to realize that he is, and always has been, one very angry man. Although not necessarily for the reasons that he cites.

Okay, the anger piece does not fit with the Cinderella story. But, as every emotionally abused woman soon discovers, Mr Nasty doesn't feel any particular need to be consistent. Or even honest.

This is why Mr Nasty sees himself as the Prince, as well as a Cinderella figure.

Curiously enough, it is usually when Mr Nasty is having a field day, giving expression to all his nastiest feelings, that he reminds his partner that he is a Prince. There is a fine irony in the fact that Mr Nasty will always tell his partner how very lucky she is to have him precisely when his behavior is thoroughly horrible.

Stranger still, although a woman realizes now that Mr Nasty is behaving extraordinarily badly, part of her will still buy that Prince line. She will actually parrot to herself the notion that she is incredibly lucky to have him because, for all his nastiness and bad behavior, he is, indeed, truly wonderful.

Admittedly, she may find it hard to reconcile Mr Nasty with the good things she loved about her partner in the early days of the relationship. However, that won't stop her from having a damned good try.

Emotionally abused women are loyal to a fault. They manage to focus on and take comfort from every good quality—whether great or small—that their Mr Nasty has ever shown. They continue to remember every last good quality—even if it hasn't been on display for longer than they care to remember.

**And, of course, they blame themselves.**

If he has turned from this *"wonderful (if hurt) man"* into a raging demon, then it must be their fault. Mustn't it?

There is just one small flaw in an abused woman's argument. Here it is:

**There are women up and down the country, and across every continent, who are also living with dead ringers for Mr Nasty.**

Their Mr Nasty may be:

- Fatter or thinner
- Younger or older
- Richer or poorer
- More, or less, macho
- More attractive, or uglier
- More, or less, articulate
- White, brown, black, or honey-colored
- More, or less, educated

There is no need to create an exhaustive description of Mr Nasty. Different Mr Nasties in different countries may show slight regional variations. However, the bottom line is this: Every Mr Nasty is a clone.

No Mr Nasty is an individual. No Mr Nasty is really interested in working to heal his own pain, and to grow up. They are all, essentially, two-year-olds having a raging temper tantrum. Yet they have all the verbal, and mental, sophistication of an adult.

That is why Mr Nasty can hurt his partner so much. It also explains, in part, why he manages to keep hooking his partner in—she simply cannot make sense of what she is seeing.

As you read through the book, you will notice that I do not always call that clone *"Mr Nasty"* in what follows. Often, I use his rightful titles: *"abusive man," "abusive partner," "abusive husband." "Mr Nasty"* describes his temperament very effectively; the adjective *"abusive"* is the only accurate description of his behavior.

**The purpose of this book** is to help you understand what happened to you, how to spot other abusers a mile off, and how you can heal from your abusive relationships.

Because all abusers—essentially—sing from the same hymn sheet, they all inflict the same kind of damage on their partners. Which means that our healing processes will be similar.

I've spent years refining everything I have learnt about abuse recovery, in order to help women escape as quickly and painlessly as possible from the destructiveness of *"Abuse World."* The next part of that work is rehabilitation so that they can feel safe and confident to build healthy relationships.

This book should provide you with a useful starting point. By the time you have finished reading it, you will understand the mechanisms that an abusive man uses to control you.

If you feel you would benefit from more support and clarity along your healing journey, then working with me may be just what you need. If you need help actually applying all that you have read, or feel overwhelmed by the difficulties you face, or are simply in a hurry to transform your situation, in the shortest possible time, then personalized help may well be your best way forward.

Whatever Mr Nasty said you could never be, do, or have in a life without him, he lied. Understanding how he operates and detaching emotionally from him are powerful first steps along the road to recovery.

Warm wishes for your healing journey,

*Annie*

# Solutions

You've probably come here looking for answers and solutions.

Answers you will surely find—answers to questions like:

- "How could he?"
- "Will he change?"
- "Why does he treat me like that?"
- "Is he really abusive?"

…and many more.

Solutions may be a little more difficult.

Why?

Because you already *know* exactly what you need to do. That's not the problem, at all.

The problem is finding the courage to do it. The problem is getting to the point of really believing that, when you walk away, you will **NOT** regret it. Trust me, you will **NOT** be walking away from the best man you are ever likely to find. *(Even if you never have another relationship with a man in your life, your abusive partner is still bad news, and best **out of your life**.)*

But that is a hard thing to take on board. It's hard to let go of all the love and hope you have invested in someone who is unworthy of you.

That's why it will be helpful to read through this book, and only then turn to the chapter entitled "Next Steps."

I believe that you will do what is right for you. Despite what you may feel right now, I have no doubt that you will find the strength and courage to start to **love yourself first** and focus on building a life that supports and nurtures you, instead of settling for emotional crumbs as you do now.

If you are not ready yet, that is okay. Please don't worry about it. That day will surely come.

And if you decide that you need personal support to help you move forward, that is perfectly understandable, given the experiences that you have endured.

But first, read the book. Then take it from there.

# #Metoo—Outing emotional abuse

My client had just discovered that her work had been favorably reviewed in one of the most prestigious papers in the land. She was over the moon. I was over the moon for her.

But that moment of joy came after 6 weeks of agony. Until then, it had looked as if her work had fallen into the void. She had told herself that the critics all hated her work. Her work had been her last hope of showing up in the world as a worthwhile human being. Her work, alone, stood between her being a failure as a human being and having some reason to live. Suicide had been very much on her mind.

If you were to meet my client, none of this would make sense to you. She is beautiful, bright and funny. She is articulate and creative. She is also an incredibly charming person. Plus, she has all the social graces in spades.

But that is not how she sees herself. In her own eyes, she is someone to be pitied. She sees herself as a lonely, pathetic, unlovable figure with nothing to say for herself. She sees herself as odd - crazy even - and unlovable.

That is the skewed perspective born of a long experience of emotional abuse. That is the skewed perspective that this book will enable you to acknowledge. Plus, if that perspective resonates with you, as a survivor of emotional abuse, this book will encourage you to offer yourself the self-compassion that you deserve, so that you can, finally, start to move beyond your damaging experiences.

Over the past 15 years, I have worked with the victims of emotional abuse across 4 continents. I have worked with women from different cultural and religious backgrounds. However, the one thing that does not change is the effect that emotional abuse has had on their lives.

For too long, we have treated emotional abuse as a problem for the individual on the sharp end of it. In some countries at least, we are beginning to realize that its more in-your-face close relative, domestic violence, is a problem for society, also. But we do not truly understand the cost to society of emotional abuse.

A lot of people do not even know where *"banter"* ends and emotional abuse begins. *"Sticks and stones"* the old adage goes, *"may break my bones, but words will never harm me."* It is hard to know who could formulate such a statement, if not some life-form that had no contact with human beings.

Words, after all, change the world—for better and for worse. Martin Luther King could hardly have advanced the Civil Rights movement without words. Without words, Adolf Hitler would have struggled to persuade his followers to commit genocide. We should never underestimate the power of words.

Those of us who have experienced emotional abuse in our lives from family and/or an intimate partner need to own this one fact—*something toxic happened to us*. People who were meant to love and cherish us, did no such thing. Instead, they made us feel despicable.

Of course, they would deny that what they did was despicable. *How could they not?* They belong to the race of people who believe that denying the harm that they do clears them of all responsibility and shifts all blame onto you.

You have carried *their* shame for too long.

Instead of continuing to carry *their* shame and feel ashamed of the way you feel, the time has come for you to understand how their attitude has generated your painful feelings.

Until we can accept that we have those feelings, until we can actually articulate them and say, *"Yes, this is how I feel"*, we cannot liberate ourselves from them. So, let us take an overview at the—*inevitable*—effects on all of us who have experienced emotional abuse from a loved one.

1)  We feel unlovable.

2)  We carry a lot of guilt.

3)  We are bowed down by shame.

4)  We tell ourselves that our lives are - effectively - over. We are too broken ever to be whole again.

5)  We blame ourselves for everything.

6)  We expect bad things to happen to us.

7)  We lack resilience.

8)  We try to compensate for our own lack of protection by protect everyone else.

9)  We get into bad relationships.

10)  We stay in bad relationships.

11)  We let people walk all over us.

12)  We apologize for everything.

13)  We find it difficult to trust the right people.

14)  We find ourselves trusting exactly the wrong people.

15) We try to compensate for the love and closeness that we never had.

16) We struggle with boundaries.

17) We are out of touch with ourselves. So out of touch with ourselves that we believe an abuser's absurd assertion that they know us better than we know ourselves.

18) We are terrified of making mistakes.

19) We live in constant fear of being punished.

20) We are dogged by the fear of regret.

21) We try to be perfect.

22) We people-please like crazy.

23) We feel like we are going crazy.

24) We desperately seek other people's good opinion.

25) We deprioritize ourselves and our health.

26) We accept bad behavior.

27) We are easily paralyzed by fear.

28) We can be hideously indecisive in our private lives.

29) We become invisible - to others and ourselves. It is as if we cease to exist.

30) We underestimate our capacities.

31) We underachieve.

32) We give up on ourselves.

33) We misdiagnose ourselves as *"crazy"*, *"needy"*, or even *"abusive"*.

34) We self-harm.

35) We use addictions to try and numb the pain.

36) We take anti-depressants and other mood-changing drugs to enable us to stay in an unbearable relationship.

37) We become suicidal.

If you recognize yourself in any of these statements, the time has come to say to yourself, *"Me too"*. You feel just like every other woman who has been through the damaging, depersonalizing experience of an emotionally abusive relationship.

An abusive partner wreaks untold havoc in a life. They teach you how to treat yourself with contempt.

What you have been through is monstrous. It's terrible and inexcusable. Nevertheless, you can come back from there. This book will teach you how to start to see yourself in the new light of the extraordinary person you really are, to hold your head up and say, *"Me too"*, with pride.

Now is the time for you to start to see the amazing, precious, courageous woman behind the abusive construct that your abuser foisted upon you.

# Two Little Words That Can Make You Feel Like A Victim

Being around an emotionally abusive partner is reason enough to make anyone feel like a victim. Unfortunately, feeling like a victim has a markedly harmful effect on a person's happiness and well-being. It gets in the way of a person feeling good *enough* about themselves to make the changes they need to make.

In this chapter, we shall look at the two little words that can make your life *even harder*, when you already feel down. But let's start by looking at exactly what we mean by the word *"victim"*.

**The 3 aspects of being a victim.**

A quick look online reveals that the word *"victim"* has three definitions, or aspects to it;

- **Aspect #1** - A person harmed, injured, or killed as a result of an event or action.

- **Aspect #2** - A person who is tricked or duped.

- **Aspect #3** - A person who has come to feel helpless and passive in the face of misfortune or ill-treatment.

All three apply to anyone unfortunate enough to have a relationship with an emotional abuser. Thankfully, only a relatively small proportion of emotionally abusive relationships end in murder. However, every emotionally abusive relationship can make you feel like death. In an emotionally abusive relationship you will undergo significant damage.

That damage *happens to you.*

Of course, an emotional abuser will always tell you that "*It*" is all your fault. He argues that the responsibility for his behavior towards you lies with you. We must assume that he, poor poppet, is so challenged by the effort of looking *(more or less)* like an adult, that we could not possibly expect him to behave like one.

Or maybe it is meant to be your fault that he *is*—and acts like—an overgrown toddler.

*Who knows? Who cares?*

The thing is, *you care*. Very much.

You feel like a victim because you have been tricked and duped by this person so often that you believe him more than you believe yourself. No wonder you end up feeling **Aspect #3** so keenly.

In an emotionally abusive relationship the abuser's ill-treatment becomes your new normal. It is absolutely normal to feel helpless, powerless and passive when that ill-treatment becomes your reality. However those feelings work to paralyze you.

Ultimately, those feelings of passiveness, powerlessness and helplessness stand in the way of you having the life and the happiness you deserve. They get channeled into two little words that distort your perceptions and make you feel like a victim.

**Just two little words.**

Can two little words really be so powerful? Do just two words have the power to catapult you into overwhelming feelings of victimhood?

Absolutely. If you need proof, think for a moment, about one, slightly bigger word, *"selfish"*, which has the power to make most women want to curl up in shame. That one, little, two syllable word exerts a MASSIVE effect. It unleashes all your shame and self-doubt. It drives you to try even harder and pay even less attention to your own needs.

Never underestimate the power that the words you and others use, have over you. If you could just turn off the volume on your abuser's words, a lot of their power over you would just evaporate. If you can just eliminate the two little words that you may well use rather a lot, without even realizing that you do, you will start to feel stronger, more resilient and more in control of your world.

So what are the two little words that you—just like everyone else in a similar situation—use that make you feel like a victim?

*"To me."*

**Be careful not to take ownership of the bad stuff that happens to you.**

It is normal to ask why someone that you love behaves that badly to you. It is understandable to ask, "How can he do that *to me?*" Nevertheless, that *"to me"* tacked onto to the end of a question, or observation, sucks.

Simply by tagging the *"to me"* onto the end of your questions about his behavior, you personalize your experience. That *"to me"* serves to make his behavior somehow about you.

When you omit those two little words and ask, instead, *"How could he behave so badly?"* and *"How could he speak like that?"* the questions elicit answers of a very different order. Answers that fit *that* bill include:

- Quite easily.
- He has a vile temper.
- That's just the way he is *(when he is not trying to impress people).*
- He gets it from his father/mother.
- Because he is an out-and-out jerk.

All of these are, likely, true. He does what he does because he is who—and what—he is. He does what he does *"to you"* because you are the person closest to hand. Nobody else is as likely to tolerate his behavior—and still try to love him into being a nicer person than he ever intends to be.

31

It is inevitable that an emotionally abusive partner will continue to victimize you for as long as you tolerate them in your life—whether or not you remain, formally, in a relationship with them. That is why you really cannot allow them to exert power over your feelings. That is why you cannot afford to make their toxic behavior *towards you* a reflection on you.

You serve your own well-being and happiness when you stop feeling like a victim and stop asking yourself questions that end in *"to me"*. Don't let those two—sucky—little words make you feel like a victim ever again. People only ever do what they do *"to you"* because that is what they do. Their behavior is their responsibility—even when it happens *"to you"*.

# Two Little Words That Will Make You Hold Your Head Up High

In the previous chapter, we looked at the two little words that make you feel like a victim. So, now, it seems only right to look at the two little words that will make you hold your head up high.

An emotionally abusive relationship teaches you to hang your head in shame.

Obviously, it serves the abuser's purpose for you to hang your head in shame. That way, you spend your time looking down—both literally and metaphorically. Down at the ground and down on yourself. That does not help you.

When you are in a black hole, looking down just makes that hole look deeper, darker and more inescapable.

As a general principle, when something is not working for you, it pays to do something different. Not necessarily the opposite. Simply opting for the opposite can be a knee-jerk reaction that only leaves you *differently* stuck. What will serve you best is to see things through different eyes.

When you are in a black hole, whether or not you choose to look up is up to you. But what is really important is to think about what might lie beyond that black hole. Hence the importance of those two little words that will make you hold your head high.

Those two little words are, interestingly enough, almost the same words that can make you feel like a victim. The difference lies in the word order—plus one extra *"o"*. In this chapter, I invite you to look beyond *"to me"* to *"me, too"*. Once again. In the context of your own emotional life. Sometimes, salvation lies in turning your focus to the detail.

## The power of detail

*"To me"* thinking serves two, unfortunate purposes. First, it triggers feelings of shame and second, it triggers intense feelings of isolation and powerlessness in a given scenario.

*"Me too"*, on the other hand, stands for a powerful statement of connection. Especially in the context in which it has been recently used in the media. The #MeToo movement has, for me, been as much about transcending individual shame as it has been about outing disgraceful attitudes and behaviors.

Needless, to say, the *"me too"* concept applies just as much to the abusive *"intimate"* relationship as it does to the workplace. Not that I am suggesting that you choose this moment to go public. That is likely to require you to run a gauntlet that you really don't want or need to run right now. But I am, very much, asking you to embrace the *"me too"* concept in your own life. Here's why.

All emotional abusers seek to isolate you. *(In case you are wondering, for me, the term "emotional abuser" includes Narcissists, coercive controllers, and physically violent partners since they all, ultimate violate your sense of yourself as a worthy, equal human being.)*

## How an emotional abuser isolates you

All emotional abusers go about isolating you in two monstrously destructive ways by;

1) Alienating you from friends, family and anyone who might value you, and
2) Estranging you from your sense of yourself as someone who matters to others.

It is with that purpose of alienating and estranging you that emotional abusers resort to such tried and trusted childhood lines, as *"Everybody thinks that you are…"* and *"Nobody likes you. (Or, at least, they wouldn't if they knew what I know about you.)"*

## The effects of isolation

Every human being craves connection and struggles with disconnection. That is why we find it so hard to separate ourselves from an abusive partner. Vile as that person doubtless has been to us, they have ensured that they are the only person through whom we believe we can *"redeem"* ourselves. That was the ultimate purpose of the appalling lies they tell you like,

- *"You'll never find someone as wonderful as me."* and
- *"Nobody else would ever want you."*

An emotional abuser does everything in their power to disconnect you from the world so that they can be your world—and use you in every sick way that they choose in order to make themselves feel better.

**How you move from isolation to reconnection**

Those two little words, *"Me too"* are all about you reclaiming your connection with the human race, and especially with everyone else who has experienced what you have, too.

In my years of working with emotionally abused women, I have heard so many tragic stories—tragic in the sense that beautiful, amazing human beings have been emotionally trashed by unworthy *"partners"*. All of these women ended up feeling like social outcasts and, essentially, rejects from the human race.

Of course, the detail of these stories varies from woman to woman. But here's the deal. The *abusive experience* of being humiliated, isolated and rejected has happened to an awful lot of us. 1 in 4 women, at least, statistically speaking. Quite probably, it has happened to rather more *of us* than that, as well. After all, until very recently, women who had *"only"* experienced verbal, emotional, abuse probably would not have sought the help that would have led them to be counted in the statistics.

**You are one of many, many women**
Even if we stick with that 1 in 4 statistic, that suggests that there an awful lot of *us*. It means that you are, actually, one of many.

As I write this, I am sitting in my favorite coffee shop. It is by no means full, but there are eight women here. That means that, in all likelihood, at least two of *us* have experienced vile treatment at the hands of an intimate partner.

Obviously, we are not having a cozy chat about it. Nor am I about to introduce myself and say, *"I've been through X, Y, and Z. How about you?"* (*There are better times and places for people to bare their souls than when they are minding their own business, doing their shopping and enjoying a coffee.*)

Nevertheless, if the time and the circumstances were right for us to open up, there is a level at which at least two of us we would be attuned to each other's deep hurts. We would recognize each other as sisters in suffering.

**Things we share**

Some of the things, that we *"Me Too"* women share, include,

- Being called all sorts of vile names by our partner.

- Being made a joke of to other people.

- Being labeled useless and worthless.

- Being rejected - both emotionally and sexually.

- Being badmouthed to our children.

- Being attacked and humiliated in front of our children.

- Being violated emotionally and sexually by our "intimate partner".

- Being told that we were lucky to have someone who constantly criticized and blamed us.

- Being threatened.

- Being treated as inferiors.

- Being let down and betrayed - and then being blamed for it.

- Being intimidated so often that we have a very easily triggered cower reflex.

- Being so humiliated that we often feel like giving up on ourselves and life.

- Being made to feel unsafe so often that we wonder if we can ever feel safe again.

- Having our trust betrayed so badly that we feel that we could never trust again.

- Feeling frightened for our mental health and our life.

- 

Has that—and quite possibly, more—happened to you? Me too.

"*It*"—that is an emotionally abusive partner—has happened to me and to 1 in 4 other women. "*It*" continues to happen despite the fact that society is beginning to wake up to the ugly reality of emotional abuse and Narcissism.

Have you ever thought how many women there must be out there—including celebrities—whose *"intimate"* partner experience has been similar to yours? It puts you and me in the same category as Tina Turner, Rihanna, Halle Berry and J.K. Rowling, to name but the few who spring instantly to mind. All in all, that is a pretty classy group of women to belong to.

Your abuser did everything possible to make you feel like a human reject. But, in reality, you share your experience and your feelings with one woman in four. Me too.

You went through all of that and you are still standing *(if only just, on a bad day)*. Me too. That is no mean feat. You are awesome. You just need to own that. *(Me too.)*

# Are You A Hopium Addict?

If the question alone was enough to make you recoil in horror, it doesn't necessarily mean that the term couldn't possibly apply to you. You may not have heard the term before, but your reaction may be because you are a closet hopium addict.

**What is the definition of a hopium addict?**

*"A hopium addict is someone who puts their own emotional needs on hold while they wait for their partner to kick their addiction—be it to drugs, alcohol, gambling, or emotionally and physically abusive behavior—despite all the evidence to the contrary."*

Addiction to drugs, alcohol, and gambling are easy enough to identify. The addiction to emotionally and physically abusive behavior is generally far less readily identifiable, at least to the woman who is on the receiving end of it.

You see, **women don't intentionally fall in love with Mr Nasty**; they don't consciously give their heart to a bully. They will fall in love with someone who presents as strong, masterful, in control, masculine, powerful, resourceful, confident—in short, someone who'll "complete" them, someone who appears to embody all the old-fashioned stereotypes of what a man is. (Or at least what a man was, before the feminists started to challenge the stereotype.)

Now, the man who appears to embody all these stereotypes behaves in a particular way that allows his conquest to slip into "I'm-a-princess-and-I've-finally-been-rescued-by-my-prince" mode. Suddenly, all the burdens of coping on her own have been lifted from her shoulders. Suddenly, she'll never have to "do life" alone again...

By rights, these couples should just walk off happily into the sunset together, the man chivalrously keeping his sheathed sword at his left hip to protect his lady from danger... Except that the relationship is not really like that.

**Abusive men start out charming**, possibly chivalrous, but definitely *in control*. They tend to be fast wooers—because their veneer of confident masculinity is actually rather thin and brittle. Underlying the veneer is a profound sense of personal inadequacy and a fundamental dislike of women. (If you listen to them long enough they'll tell you how key female figures in their life have wronged them. At bottom, they mistrust all women.)

Once the fog of hormones, pheromones, and straight lust starts to lift, things play out rather differently. Abusive men seek commitment yet loathe the demands it imposes on them. They encourage their partner to depend on them, then become acutely resentful of the dependency they see.

This resentment increasingly reveals itself in reproaches, fault-finding, withdrawal of intimacy, and escalating outbursts of anger. Whether or not physical violence is used, the nature of these outbursts is violent, inasmuch as it shatters trust and undermines the woman's feelings of self-worth.

The man may, or may not, threaten to leave. Almost certainly, he will point out to his partner how fundamentally flawed and unworthy she is. The woman is likely to have difficulty reconciling this stranger, who is incandescent with self-righteous fury, with the prince who wooed her.

An attack of this kind is devastating and, at least in the early days, the woman is likely to reveal the depth of her distress. When she does so, the man's fury will subside and he will revert to being her loving cavalier... for a while at least.

The point is:

**Mr Nasty restores his own feelings of self-worth by cutting *"the little woman"* down to size**—irrespective of whatever it is that occurred to make him feel small in the first place.

But there's also a calculation involved: whether or not he loves her, he desperately needs her, because he uses her to shore up his feelings about himself. So he has to do his best not to drive her away. This is why he reverts back to loving mode... until the next time. And there always will be a next time—which will always be worse than the time before—because in order to get his payoff, he has to up the ante.

Over time, as he keeps knocking her down (psychologically and perhaps physically also), he becomes more confident that she won't leave. With all the conflict, she loses the energy and the sense of independent identity that she needs in order to leave. So the loving interludes become less necessary for him, and less frequent.

**And that's where the hopium addiction comes in.** He may still *"mainline"* her just enough love to keep her locked in; or else she may be so starved that she stays, when she should have left long ago, still trying to get the *"fix"* she needs—the fix that she misguidedly believes only he can provide.

**The hopium addict is the woman who thinks that her partner loves her *really*—**he just has difficulty showing it because he's had a hard time. She believes that somehow it will all work out all right, they'll find a way to live happily together ever after, and the kids won't be affected.

Unfortunately, hopium addiction is degenerative. Like any other addiction, unless you get treatment, it will destroy you.

# "How Can I Change My Abusive Partner?"

Questions abused women always ask me are:

- "Will he ever change?"
- "How can I make him change?"
- "What can I do to change him?"

Those questions always remind me of something my daughter said to me. Speaking with the world-weariness of the very young, she once informed me that ***"The only way you can change a man is when he is wearing a diaper."***

Precisely.

When abused women ask me these questions, they have an agenda: their agenda is to find a justification for staying with their abusive husband. If there is a hope that Mr Nasty can—and will—change someday, then they can tell themselves that they are right to stay. After all, they have invested so much in him already. Wouldn't it be disastrous to get rid of their investment just before his stock started to rise?

Well, I guess it would. Then again, that is not going to happen.

**Mr Nasty is not going to change *for you*,** because that is not his agenda. When he selected you for a partner, he selected you quite carefully. He did a few trial runs early on in the relationship to assure himself that he could visit his temper tantrums and bad behaviors on you and that you would take it.

Most likely, at the start, his temper tantrums and bad behaviors were relatively insignificant. Still, the fact remains he experimented with yelling at you, treating you badly, possibly hitting you—and you passed the test with flying colors, because you took it.

Even if you said to him, *"I don't expect to be treated that way,"* or walked away, in the end you agreed to accept it, by getting back together with him. That was how he knew that he had found someone over whom he could exert power and control, by visiting all his bad feelings on you, whenever he chose.

***Why on earth would he ever put himself to the trouble of changing for you?***

Sure, there is Every Abused Woman's Not-So-Secret Fantasy that one day the scales will fall from his eyes with a deafening thud that will be heard as far away as China, and Mr Nasty will say, *"I'm so sorry. I've been such a fool. I really love you. Finally, I understand what I've done, and I'm going to spend the rest of my life making it up to you."*

Now, I know a number of women who have heard that pretty little speech. When they walked away from their abusive husband, he found their absence intolerable, and so cast about in his own mind until he found the right formula to fully reclaim their attention. It worked. Many went back into the relationship; some remarried the man to whom they had previously been miserably tethered. One woman I can think of got a massive diamond ring out of it.

**"Ah, but did the relationship work after they got back together?"**

No, it did not. Abusive men will raise their game and play Mr Nice Guy when they have to, but then they revert to type.

The time came when I tired sufficiently of my abusive marriage to suggest a trial separation. After the shock, the rage, and the tearfulness, the then husband reached for his thinking cap. (It wasn't very big, and he had to look long and hard to find it.)

And he had a dream. (At the time, he was paying an analyst so he could talk about his dreams, and so he assumed that everyone would be fascinated by them.) In the dream, he was in a Boeing 747 that was going to crash. Somehow, he took over from the pilot, got the plane back up to a safe altitude, and saved the passengers' lives.

A nice metaphor for the abuser rescuing the relationship that he had brought to within a hair's breadth of destruction.

Except that it did not pan out quite that way.

He did not rescue the relationship. He managed to salvage his own best interest by persuading me that he had changed. Then, naturally, he reverted to business as usual and became, if anything, even more objectionable.

**Abusive men do not ever change their character flaws to make you happy.**

They will not change for you, and they will not be changed by you. It may be possible for them to change, but they will only ever do so if for some reason they decide that their current behavior does not offer them sufficient payoffs. To all intents and purposes, the likelihood of an abuser changing massively is right up there with winning the lottery.

If, by chance, your abusive partner agrees to change, or says he has changed, be very wary. If he tells you that he needs your help to change, he is really asking you to keep on carrying him.

**And why is it that abused women are always so focused on changing their partner?**

Perhaps you haven't heard the expression, *"Change begins at home"*—at home in the sense of with you, rather than in the sense of in the home (and with him).

**The only person you can ever successfully change is yourself.**

Long and bitter experience of trying to change someone else—specifically an abusive man—may have led you to believe that change is incredibly hard work and also doomed to failure. It is, of course, when you try to change another person. You cannot pin the changes you want on another person any more than you can dress and make up the image of yourself reflected in a mirror.

**Your best chance of transforming yourself comes about when you detach completely from Mr Nasty**—because only then do you stop fighting with his construct of you, and start being yourself.

When you focus on your own transformation, and on moving forward—rather than moving back into a

slightly improved version of a toxic relationship—
change can be quick, easy, and immensely rewarding.
Especially if you have the skilled support that you need
to speed you along that journey.

# How to **Support** Friends and Loved Ones through an Abusive Relationship

This is a question that comes up a lot. It's hugely frustrating, as well as difficult and painful, to watch someone you care about struggle in the quicksand of an abusive relationship.

It's frustrating because we can see all the things that they can't. We'd love to help them—which probably means getting them to adopt the solution that we know is right. But they don't see it—and they're not going to do so.

It's difficult because you start to feel like you're caught up in Groundhog Day. They reach the point of leaving, they may well even leave... and then the whole thing goes around again and again. Maybe the same partner, maybe a different one. But you hear the same story again and again.

**In the end, your emotional investment wears you out.** You end up feeling resentful towards them for what they're putting you through.

It's painful because watching someone turn into a shadow of their former self is tragic. All the more so when there are children who are also suffering. Witnessing the pain of someone you care about and not being able to make it go away really taxes your resources.

So how do you support them?

First, **you need to be clear about the distinction between *helping* and *supporting* them.**

You cannot help them; i.e., move them on—even as much as a millimeter. What you can do is be there for them.

But that doesn't mean making yourself available to listen 100 percent of the time.

What it does mean is simply acknowledging and respecting their right to make choices or to stick with the situation. However disastrous it may appear from the outside, they are making the best choices they can at the time. They already feel pretty bad about themselves; your continued respect may make more of a difference than you could imagine.

Second, **you MUST NOT give up on them**. There is a very human temptation, at some point, to say "Whatever!" and walk away. Abusers create a void around their victim that leaves the victim even more dependent. It's very easy to end up becoming irritated with the victim. When you do, you're actually—*albeit unwittingly*—colluding with the abuser.

If an abused loved one can't hold on to the thought of life beyond their relationship, then that is something important we can do for them. This simply means believing and trusting that they will come out the other side. Even if neither of you can predict the timescale.

Third, **you can hold on to the knowledge of who they truly are**. Over time, living with a self-appointed King of the Jungle reduces them to feeling little better than a cockroach. You can hold on to—and remind them of—their gifts, their qualities, their uniqueness, and their lovableness, until they are able to do it for themselves. Your vision may be the resource that starts them on their journey to recovery.

It doesn't even have to be a major holding operation on your part. Remember, abuse leaves its victims starving because it systematically closes down any channel of nourishment. Often, by opening up a channel, you offer them more sustenance than you could possibly imagine.

To a friend of mine who had completely lost sight of herself, having suffered hugely at the hands of a homicidally brutal partner, I sent a list of the blessings that she did not see. The list is incredibly empowering for her, and she treasures it.

It reads like this:

*1) You are blessed with good and loving friends.*
*2) You inspire great love in those around you.*
*3) You have two wonderful children—they may be not easy, but they definitely are wonderful.*
*4) You have enormous strength.*
*5) You have a vast reservoir of talents.*
*6) You are an extraordinarily loving and supportive person.*
*7) You have a talent for creating beauty.*
*8) You have an extraordinarily attractive personality.*
*9) You have formidable energy.*
*10) All this and there is still, I'd guess, about another 85 percent of capacity that you are currently not able to access efficiently.*

My friend is unique and gifted. So are all our friends and loved ones. Another person's list may be different, but it will be no less extraordinary. We are all uniquely gifted and wonderful. Yet we may need to have our eyes opened to this fact. Repeatedly.

You support others best when you offer them a valid, empowering vision of themselves. You support yourself when you do the selfsame thing for yourself.

# "Sticks and Stones" – The 7 Most Important Things To Know About Mental Abuse

**1.** ***"Sticks and stones won't break my bones"***—and words won't leave any measurable physical damage, but they will cause progressive, long-term harm. Never underestimate the power of words; words are used to brainwash.

Being told you are *"stupid," "ugly," "lazy,"* or *"worthless"* is never acceptable. The first times you hear it, it will hurt, naturally. In time you may "get used to" hearing it from a partner. That is when you start to internalize and believe it.

When that happens, you are doing the other person's work—of putting you down—for them. This is why your feelings of self-worth suffer increasingly over time.

The good news is that, just as words have been used to bring you down, you can learn to harness the power of words to build yourself up and restore your confidence and self-belief.

**2. You are always told that it's your fault.** Somehow, whatever happens, however it starts, the ultimate blame is always yours. Notice that we are talking ultimate blame here. The blaming partner will always tell you that their behavior was caused by what you said or did. In fact, their argument runs along the lines that you can't possibly blame them for anything, because if you hadn't said what you said, or done what you did, it would never have happened.

**3. You're more inclined to believe your partner than you are to believe yourself.** Have you ever reeled with a sense of hurt and injustice, or seethed with anger at the way you've been treated? Have you found yourself asking, *"Is it reasonable to feel like this?" "Am I misinterpreting things?" "Have I got it wrong?"*?

If this is you, what it means is that you have become so brainwashed that you have stopped trusting your own judgment. Your mind keeps throwing up observations and questions because, deep down, you know that what is happening is utterly wrong. But, right now, you can't feel the strength of your own convictions.

**4. You need your partner to acknowledge your feelings.** Have you ever felt desperate to make your partner hear what you are saying and apologize for the hurtful things they have said? Have you ever felt that only they can heal the pain they have caused?

Does your need for them to validate your feelings keep you hooked into the relationship?

When a partner constantly denies or refuses to listen to your feelings, that is, unquestionably, mental abuse.

**5. Your partner blows hot and cold.** He can be very loving but is often highly critical of you. He may tell you how much he loves you, yet he is short on care or consideration towards you. In fact, some of the time, maybe even a lot of the time, he treats you as if you were someone he truly dislikes.

You do everything you can to make him happy, but it's never good enough. You're more like the pet dog in the relationship than you are the equal partner. Your constant efforts to get his attention and please him meet with limited success. Sometimes he'll be charmed; often he's dismissive.

If you find yourself puzzling about how your partner can treat you that way, it is because you are trying to live in a love-based relationship, when in reality you are living in a control-based relationship. The mental abuser struggles with his own feelings of worthlessness and uses his relationship to create a feeling of personal power, at his partner's expense.

**6. You feel as if you are constantly walking on eggshells.** There is a real degree of fear in the relationship. You have come to dread his outbursts, the hurtful things that he will find to say to you. *(Maybe the same anxiety and need to please spill over into your other relationships also.)*

***Fear is not part of a loving relationship.*** But fear is a vital part of a mentally abusive relationship. It enables the abuser to maintain control over you.

**7. You can heal.** Mentally abusive relationships cause enormous emotional damage to the loving partner who tries, against all odds, to hold the relationship together but ultimately can't do it because her partner is working against her.

Whether you are currently in a mentally abusive relationship, have left one recently, or years later are still struggling with the anxieties, low self-worth, and lack of confidence caused by mental abuse, it is never too late to heal.

But you do need to work with a person, and a program, that focus specifically on mental-abuse recovery.

Women who have suffered mental abuse expect radical change of themselves, and they expect it right away. This is why they often struggle and, not uncommonly, why they take up with another abusive partner.

Mental-abuse recovery is a gradual process. Low self-worth and limiting beliefs about what kind of future the abuse sufferer can ever hope for are the blocks that can stop women from moving on. But they are blocks that you can clear very effectively, provided you have specialist help.

Language was once used to harm you. Happily, you can learn how language can heal you. You can discover how to overcome past mental abuse and keep yourself safe from it in the future. You can also learn to feel strong, believe in yourself and create the life and the relationships you truly want.

Whether or not sticks and stones have broken your bones, words can one day heal you.

# 16 Ways to Spot an Abusive Man

Women constantly ask me, *"How can I avoid making the same mistake again? If I could get it so horribly wrong with my abusive ex, how can I be sure that I won't do the same thing again?"*

The question is an important one. We are likely to be—*unconsciously* but powerfully—drawn to the same personality type that we first encountered in an abusive parent or sibling. Or else, we opt for someone who appears to be the polar opposite of our ex – only to find that beneath the vulnerable, adoring façade an abuser still lurks. In this chapter we shall look at 16 pointers that you will need to make sense of, *for yourself.*

1. **You may be attracted by his apparent *"strength," "confidence,"* determination, aggressive masculinity**—the kinds of qualities you know you lack.

2.  **Or it may be his vulnerability that appeals.**
    Maybe his Little-Boy-Hurt routine tugs at your
    oh-so empathetic heartstrings. You might find
    yourself saying, *"He just needs someone to really, really
    love him (and heal his pain)."* Why does it need to be
    you? Feeling sorry for someone is no basis for a
    loving relationship of equals.

(Note: **Your focus has shifted from you—your wants
and your needs—to him and his. He has replaced
you as the center of your universe.**)

3.  **At the beginning of the relationship, he really,
    really wants to hear about all the problems
    you're having.** He may even have the same
    problems himself. (Be very wary—he may be
    doing one of two things: he may be learning all
    about your Achilles' heel and the best buttons to
    push in the future to humiliate and control you;
    or he may be encouraging you to feel emotionally
    dependent on him since he, at least, understands
    what you are going through.)

4.  **He expects a big return on his investment.** He
    may seem happy to put your needs and wishes
    first for a little while, but it won't be long before
    he starts saying, *"Look at everything I do for you. You
    should be doing X, Y and Z for me."*

5. **The relationship moves forward very fast.** (Abusive men woo as fast as they can. They know that they can't sustain consistent good behavior for very long. Good behavior doesn't give them the payoffs they want.)

6. **He talks at length—and, possibly, interestingly—about himself.** You share a common interest: him.

7. **The women who he has had relationships with in the past didn't understand him, and either let him down or behaved badly.** *(Be afraid.)* If at all possible, you want to meet these women and hear their points of view. If he can badmouth them, can you be sure that you won't be next?

8. **His relationship with his family has broken down.** They may have let him down too.

9. **There are areas of his life that he is not telling you about.** (Rest assured, there is a good reason for that.)

10. **He has got a history of alcohol and/or drug abuse, and possibly violence.**

11. **When you first meet him, there's something about him that you don't like.** (You can do it

the hard way, or the easy way. Choose not to trust your intuition and you'll probably pay for it. Big time. Your intuition is there to keep you safe.)

12. **He is all sweetness and light with you, but he shows quite different behaviors with other people.** (Rest assured that, with time, you will become *"other people".*)

13. **There are odd *"blips"* when his behavior leaves you feeling that you're dealing with someone you don't even know.** (The *"good"* behaviors that you like are his best—or courting—behaviors. The *"blips"* are an indication of his real self and what the future will increasingly hold.)

14. **He can always find reasons for not spending time with your friends and family.** He may try to discourage you from spending time with them also. The more he can isolate you, the more power he will have over you.

15. **He's not happy to accept you the way you are.** (Maybe that is because he can see all your *"potential"* better than you can. Maybe it's because, with his input, you could present yourself so much better to the world—according to him, anyway.)

16. **He will remind you regularly what a wonderful guy he is, and how lucky you are to have him.** (Although he might also admit that he's a loser when he's feeling low, or when he needs to get you back onside.)

*If you have any doubts that your partner may be or may become abusive, take the relationship slowly and listen to the advice of friends and family whose judgment you can trust. If you don't like what they say and find yourself replying, "But you don't understand. He's not like that..." the chances are that you are wrong and they are right.*

Any of the above should be considered an important warning sign.

If you hear **ANY** alarm bells going in your head, listen to them carefully and act on them right away.

The damage an abusive relationship causes is cumulative. You cannot ever make an abusive relationship work by tolerating abuse and trying to love your partner into wholeness. But you will drain yourself physically, emotionally, and spiritually.

It is quite possible to break away from the hooks of abusive relationships, although it can be very hard to do so without help. Enlisting the help of someone who understands and is skilled at helping women work their way through the problems of an abusive relationship will really speed your recovery.

# How I Found the Courage to Leave

Let's be very clear about this: like many, many other abused women, I did **not** have the courage to leave. My route out of an abusive marriage was indirect.

I spent years fantasizing about leaving, often wanting desperately to leave, but never daring to do so. I hated myself for my lack of courage, while my then husband knew it was something else he could use to humiliate me.

In those days **I didn't understand about patterns and contracts in relationships.** My ex-husband and I got together at a time when I was struggling. It's a common story. He rescued me. At the time I believed that being rescued was my best-case scenario.

**I didn't know that rescue tends to come at a very high price.** Nor did I know that dealing with the difficulties would have been more painful in the short term, but hugely empowering over the medium and long term.

*In the best of all possible worlds*, a rescuer would step in, help you through the immediate difficulty and then give you the space and the support to get back on your feet. Most rescuers don't operate like that. Most abusive men who "rescue" damsels in distress run a different program, a program whereby they win and you lose.

Mr Nasty will rescue you in the first instance, so that you will then feel obligated to rescue him for ever after. But that's not all.

As an abusive man, Mr Nasty is not remotely interested in helping you get back on your feet; he is interested in keeping you dependent. He is also extremely good at it—it's a key life skill for him. This is why abused women find it so hard to leave. Abusive men reinforce your feelings of weakness *(and self-loathing)* every time they throw your weakness back in your face. *(And, boy, do they throw it back in your face!)*

**What led me to leave was a painting.**

Maybe it only happened because I could never have predicted the course of events, never have seen it coming.

It happened like this: after over 20 years in my miserable marriage, I fell madly in love one day with a painting I saw in—of all places—a kitchen shop in Rome.

At the time, I was training full-time as an Alexander Technique teacher and had almost no income coming in. My self-worth was at an all-time low when I saw a painting that really "spoke" to me. (It still does.) I knew I had to have it. The then husband, a highly paid professional, asked me how I was going to pay for it. I replied that I would sell a few pieces of old furniture that I owned.

It's a long story but I sold the furniture, started clearing clutter from my home, and the last and best thing I cleared was the then husband. The painting remains among my most treasured possessions, both because of its own beauty and because of all that it symbolizes.

**I discovered that my courage and self-worth had been eroded** over the years by an abusive relationship *(I truly hadn't known)*. I now use all that I have learned to help other women along their road to healing and self-worth.

I now have a life I truly love that fulfils and challenges me and takes me in directions I would never have imagined, whereas before I was merely *"tiptoeing through life to arrive safely at death."*

What I have learned, and what I now teach, is that courage may be that big leap in the dark, or it may not. If you have been really beaten down by life, as many people are, then courage is a process. The beauty of it is that you only have to start the process, wherever and however you can, and a domino effect will ensue. It really doesn't matter how small your first steps are; the knock-on effect will be powerful and beneficial beyond anything that you can imagine at the start.

Nor is courage necessarily something that you have to ramp up when you feel scared out of your head. For me it started when that painting fed into a passion I have always had for Italy and all things Italian.

If someone could have told me how things would pan out just before I set foot in that shop, I would have laughed in disbelief. And yet...

I guess that courage was given to me, in the measure that I've needed it, all along the way, when I trusted the stirrings of my heart.

I believe that **courage will be given to *you*, also**. Just be warned: courage feels a lot like fear.

Courage is a label that defines outcomes rather than feelings. Don't ever sell yourself short again by believing that you can't be courageous because you don't feel courageous.

It's a myth that you need courage before you can make big changes in your life. You don't need courage at all. You just need to heed the promptings of that small inner voice, no matter whether of passion or self-preservation, and take the small steps that you can. Trust that voice and bear in mind that it will set you on a road that leads you somewhere far better than where you are stuck right now.

# My Story

A woman e-mailed me wanting to know more about my story. She wanted to hear it because she felt it might help her. When I stopped to think about it, I came to the conclusion that my story might well serve many other women. So here goes.

**I met my husband at a time in my life when I was at a low ebb emotionally**. My family of origin had always been dysfunctional and at that point there was massive conflict going on. I was in the 16-to-24-year-old age group, the age when young women are most likely to fall for an abusive man.

My future husband seemed to offer me a way forward. Although I could see that he was in some ways a very wounded young man with significant issues of his own, I felt he had strengths that I needed.

I also thought I could heal him with my love.

**Our relationship became serious and exclusive very fast**. Within a few months he had become the center of my world, and my family was excluded. Somehow I also reduced the time I spent with my friends.

**We settled into a kind of unspoken contract**. I took care of his creature comforts and subordinated my ambitions to his, and he became my *"protector."*

Because I was—*we* were—so in love at that time, it wasn't hard for me to give up my dream of going to Japan for a year to work with children.

**The first major glitch** occurred a few months into our relationship. Before then he had put me on a pedestal *(although he was less charitable about other people)*. Then one day, out of a clear-blue sky, he became very angry and accusatory. It passed after an hour or so.

During that hour, something inside me suggested that I should just walk away. But already I was terrified of losing the best boyfriend I'd ever had. Besides, I could justify staying with him because I *"loved him"*.

Within a couple of months we were married. My parents opposed the marriage so violently that they told me to choose between them and him. I didn't even have to think about it. I chose him.

**The first major flare-up occurred on our honeymoon**. A propos of nothing in particular, he stopped speaking to me.

After 24 hours of stony silence, in utter desperation I attempted suicide. I failed because the tablets I had ingested in significant quantities were designed not to be toxic. *(I hadn't known that.)*

When we made up, I thought something had been learnt and something would change.

It did. The next time my husband retreated behind a wall of silence, it lasted three days. This time I drank myself into a stupor.

By now, **a voice inside my head was telling me that the relationship was over**. I couldn't understand how or why. I was terrified of looking like a fool and leaving a marriage that was only a few months old. I also felt I had nowhere to go and nobody to turn to. So I silenced that voice and I stayed.

Naturally, my rational brain could make a good case for staying: he was such a wonderful man; he was just *hurt*; he didn't mean any harm; there was so much love, so much potential....

Maybe it was another two months before his next *"inexplicable behavior."* This time, he began with a long silence and ended it with fury and harsh criticisms. *(I had given up taking pills and alcohol by now. Instead, I just endured it, paralyzed with misery.)*

It ended with me crying my eyes out, mutual apologies and promises that it wouldn't happen again.

Of course it did, on a regular basis. And he started to talk about getting out.

**The more he talked about leaving, the more desperate I became to make him stay.** I kept remembering how much I loved him and the good times we had had together. I kept vowing to try harder.

And so it went on for years and years. The times between the explosions grew shorter, the criticisms harsher, the reconciliations less touching, but still there was that *"potential"* that I could not bear to throw away. Besides, only he had the power to make me feel good about myself. *(Not that he did, of course.)*

When I had my daughter, and became even more dependent financially and emotionally, he became still more critical.

**He projected a wonderful myth of the more competent, caring parent.** While I was constantly struggling to hold on to the last vestiges of my strength and my sanity, he seemed good-natured and patient around my daughter. (It was only later that I learned from her that that *"act"* dropped as soon as I was not around to witness it.)

I became worried that I wasn't fit to care for my own child. I certainly didn't think I could do it alone.

And so it continued. Among his other accomplishments, he added a talent for spoiling every occasion that my daughter and I enjoyed.

Once, that led to a trial separation, which lasted a few months. He sweet-talked me, told me how much he now realized he loved me, and vowed to be better if I would only help him and take him back.

I did, and for a couple of months it really was better. Mr Nice Guy was in residence. And then Mr Nasty came back with a vengeance. Once again he upped his game.

The crunch came when he took me to Venice for a landmark birthday and reached a new pitch of awfulness.

At that point I knew I had to get out or disintegrate. There was no other option. If I did not get out then, I knew I would never, ever have the strength again. I would have been his to use and abuse exactly as he wanted. It really was a *"get out or die"* moment.

Even *I* could not ignore that voice in my head.

Terrified as I was, I got out.

Initially it was agonizingly hard. All my energies were consumed by the struggle to make sense of what had happened, and to survive so that I could be a halfway good parent to my daughter.

Everything grew progressively easier over time.

**Life became far, far better than I could ever have imagined**. I discovered he had lied (yet again) when he told me that life without him would be worthless.

Now, it is my mission to do everything I can to make that healing journey as easy and swift as possible for other abused women.

Writing this, I'm shocked by what that *"past me"* went through. I'm shocked because generally I no longer remember it—and it no longer matters. My life now is rich and full.

Yours can be too.

Follow the steps to healing, and the trauma of your abusive relationship will become exactly what it should be: ancient history.

# How Can You "Rewrite" Old Trauma?

One of the many joys of the life I live now is that I am free to learn, and believe, what I choose.

**The ex-husband *(wasband)*, like all abusive men, was a firm believer in thought control.** *(Had he had his way he would have been the dictator of a banana republic, rather than one small family and one decidedly unimpressed pedigree pooch.)* Given half a chance he would have poured scorn on the skills and knowledge I have acquired since his departure. The contempt he always showed for ideas other than his own was his way of acknowledging how powerful those ideas might be.

A while back now, I was exposed to one of the most powerful ideas I have yet come across. Its formal name is *"Matrix Reimprinting."* What this actually means is that, using the right techniques, you can revisit an old trauma and rewrite that scenario in a constructive way.

Back in the bad old days of my marriage, I would have balked at this idea; rewriting your past was, I thought, the first step down the road to fantasy and losing touch with reality.

But here's the thing: **the past is old history**. It has been and gone. You suffered at the time. You have suffered since. More than enough, I would say. Now it's time for you to let the trauma go, and create something that nurtures you.

By now you may be thinking, *"What is this woman talking about?"*

Let me explain by sharing my experience with you.

At this workshop, we were asked to remember an old traumatic feeling. The feeling I chose was, *"I am insignificant."*

Having spent rather too long in an abusive marriage, I had spent a LOT of time feeling insignificant. So much so—that I could not remember any specific occasion.

Then a brief scenario from my honeymoon sprang unbidden to my mind.

The then husband had had his first full-blown abusive outburst on our honeymoon. (I recount the full story in My Story.) Mr Nasty suddenly burst onto the scene with a vengeance. In despair, I tried to kill myself. But in my ignorance, I consumed a substantial quantity of tranquillizers. They left me decidedly groggy and, happily, still alive.

I spent a whole day flaked out on the hotel bed unable to move, while my bridegroom sulked and snarled his way through the streets of Paris. Eventually he returned, observed my sorry state and, quite unmoved, got me dressed and marched me out for dinner.

There were many, many unpleasant feelings attached to that episode. But did I feel insignificant, given the circumstances?

You bet I did. Being told by my new husband, a doctor, that the episode was no big deal because I didn't have a cat's chance in hell of killing myself with the drugs I had taken, didn't make me feel that I was desperately important to him.

So there I was, that morning at the workshop, using the Matrix Reimprinting technique as I went through that old memory once again.

What happened?

In essence, using that technique, I went back into that hotel room, back to the young woman I once was, and spoke to her. I told her about the joys that lay ahead of her, the meaning she would find in her life, the capacity to love and be loved she would discover. I told her that she would never have to be so alone again, because I would always be there for her.

Then **I experienced a huge mental shift.**

First, I saw that I had married my husband and stayed with him because I had been so emotionally empty that I had needed him to do for me what I could not do for myself. I had settled for crumbs of love because in those days I could not even provide crumbs for myself.

As I realized that, **the whole trauma stopped being about him and became about me.**

Back then I hadn't known how to fill up that vast empty void. Now I do.

This was the point at which I started to rewrite the experience of that younger me. Instead of the vision of that young woman who was so heavily sedated she could barely lift her head from the hotel bed, I saw a young woman who had gained an inner assurance that she was safe and supported.

She was also loved and lovable.

Far from being nailed to her bed by misery and medication, this transformed young woman was smiling with delight at her youth and freshness as she threw her head back, like that immortal Rita Hayworth moment in Gilda.

And where was the then husband in all of this?

*He wasn't there.*

That was the beauty of the work I did. He wasn't there because **he was no longer relevant**.

I had married the then husband because that was the best I could possibly do at the time.

And he was no longer important.

I had stepped out of the old victim thinking once and for all. He really did not matter when I replayed that old scenario, *because I had finally learned the lessons of that experience and I could move on.*

# Was I Married To Your Husband?

As I often joke to a friend of mine, who had been married and divorced three times by the time she was 40, I only made the one mistake, but I made it in depth, over a couple of decades.

So I am quite clear about who I *was* married to; and I can say, with confidence, that he was one dubious pleasure that other women should have been spared.

Still, emotionally abused women ask me all the time, *"Were you married to my husband?"* Because my ex-husband sounds so much like their own abusive partner.

Now, my *was*band is a physician and a cyclist, who sometimes abused alcohol but does not have substance addictions of any kind. He is a bright, articulate Antipodean, and the child of two concentration-camp survivors.

In terms of the facts, he may be very different from your own abusive partner. In terms of behavior and temperament, I'm guessing my Mr Nasty is quite similar to your Mr Nasty.

**My Mr Nasty was controlling** *(although he could never be bothered to check up on me, as some abusive men do).*

**He was punitive** and much given to sabotaging any good moments I enjoyed.

**He hated women in general**, and me in particular.

**He seethed with a deep sense of not being good enough** and put me down to make himself feel better; and then he told me I would never find anyone as good as him again.

As I have since found out, **he was lousy at reading the future**, and wrong in his predictions, but he was very persuasive, and much given to making dire prognostications—about my future, naturally.

**He habitually used words to humiliate and hurt**, but he could do quite a nice line in passive aggression, too.

**He flew into what appeared to be uncontrolled rages**, but they were not; he was calculating enough not to overstep the limits he had set himself.

**He was an obnoxious, damaging, destructive man,** and when he thought he might have gone too far, he told me how much he loved me.

He told me that he loved me, but he acted in ways that neither showed love, nor suggested that my best interests mattered to him at all.

**He was callous and complained consistently** about how I hurt his feelings.

**He withheld love** and reproached me for being needy.

**He was unappreciative** of all that I did and told me endlessly how I disappointed him.

And I told myself—and the world—that I loved him, he was a good man really; but he had just *"had a hard time."*

**He taught me that his having had a hard time gave him the right to give me a hard time.** *(He had learnt—from his parents—how to create a chain of misery down the generations. His parents had suffered greatly, and that, in their minds, entitled them to be, at best, careless of other people's suffering. As my husband saw it, whatever hard time I may have had, it was never going to be anywhere near as hard as his hard time. My hard time did not matter. It never gave me the rights he had, to "dump" bad feelings, whenever and however he liked.)*

Of course, this is an appallingly destructive belief that abusers translate into appalling behavior. Having suffered does not give anyone the right to visit suffering on another person. Ever. But The Abusive Kingdom is a place *"red in tooth and claw."* It is a place where bad feelings confer the right to harm, rather than the responsibility to heal.

In his own eyes, my husband's hard time gave him the right not to care about the misery he caused.

**Does he sound familiar?**

Abusive men are much more like one another than they are like anyone else.

Their behavior is **not your fault**.

You do them, and yourself, no favors at all when you tolerate their bad behavior. Indulging them serves only to reward them for behaving like spoilt children. If anything, it encourages them to become even worse. Rather, as *chronological* adults, it is for *them*—not us—to take responsibility for their own behavior. No matter how much they may tell us that *their* bad behavior is your fault, that does not make it true.

You do yourself no favors when you make excuses for them. Interestingly, you stop doing so when you realize

that your partner is not so much a *"tortured individual"* as an ill-tempered, immature—and torturing—clone.
I was never married to your husband, nor you to mine—happily for both of us. But we have both *"been there, done that, and sported the same T-shirt."*

How wonderful that we can always make the decision not to be *"fashion victims"* any longer.

# 7 Things I Wish I'd known When I Started Out On The Road To Recovery

1. **The dire predictions my abusive partner made** for and about me were all completely wrong. *(Somehow, it took me the longest time to realize that he had no talent at all for predicting the future.)* As a general rule, people who make a point of predicting your future are utterly useless at it.

2. **The dire predictions that *I* made proved to be wrong.** We base our predictions for the future on the past. If you choose to stay in an abusive relationship, then of course all you can expect is more of the same. But once you start the process of change by leaving that relationship, you create a climate in which everything can change, generally for the better.

3. **My worst fears behaved every bit as badly as you would expect** worst fears to behave,

snarling and snapping and generally living up to their job description. *(Worst fears tend to be ever so conscientious.)*

Discovering acronyms of fear helped:
- **F**alse **E**vidence **A**ppears **R**eal made a dent in the power of fear.
- **F**alse **E**xpectations **A**bout **R**eality, and
- **F**uture **E**vents **A**ppearing **R**eal made me realize just how limited and inaccurate fear predictions are.
- While **F**\*\*k **E**verything **A**nd **R**un served as a graphic explanation of how my fears affected me.

4.     **There has always been help, support, love, friendship, and kindness** available to me. The only thing was, I often wrongly anticipated who it would come from. Some women friends suddenly saw me as a *femme fatale* determined to run off with their luscious man, and shied away from me. Somehow there wasn't an opportunity to tell them that:

   a)     I would sooner join a nunnery than contemplate spending time alone with their husband.

   b)     I had no intention of compounding the mess I was in by rushing into another relationship, especially one that would hurt someone I cared about.

Other people, women and men, extended a selfless kindness and consideration to me that I would never have imagined. I still remain thankful for it, thankful that they *"held"* me with their generosity when I felt like I was drowning.

5.   **Past performance is no indication of future achievement**. When my daughter was six or seven, I took her to see the musical *Me and My Girl*. Her favorite lines in it came when the aspiring, penniless hero is offered a bowl of soup and asks, *"What kind of soup is this?"* *"Bean soup,"* is the reply. Without missing a beat, he asks, *"I don't care what it's been; what is it now?"*

6.   **Life doesn't care what you've been**. Life only cares what you choose to be now. As Henry Ford said, *"If you think you can do a thing or think you can't do a thing, you're right."* Since you will be proved right, what would you like to be proved right about? What would you choose to be proved right about? Future unhappiness? Or your chance to reveal your inner extraordinariness to yourself and the world?

7.   **The best lies ahead, not behind you**. Mr Nasty is by no means stupid. At some level he knows that he wouldn't see you for dust if you had any idea how much happier your life would be without him. So he does a great job of

brainwashing you into thinking that life without him would be all downhill. In fact, he is so good at it that it can take a while after the relationship has ended to realize how manipulative and just plain wrong he was.

8.     **You're never so broken that you cannot become whole again**. Abused women massively underestimate their own resources and their capacity to heal. In my experience, they are quick learners: once they grasp the true nature of the abusive relationship and how to "do" change successfully, they start to make up for lost time, transforming themselves out of all recognition.

Providing women with the tools to make that transformation and witnessing their evolution never ceases to fill me with wonder: wonder at abused women's resilience and also wonder that I have come far enough to be able to help and support other women along their healing journey.

# Beware The Pedestal

Almost invariably, abused women revisit the early days of their relationship with regret. That was the time when their partner, in his pre-Mr Nasty incarnation, put them on a pedestal.

Boy, it felt good to be on that pedestal!

If you have rarely felt special in months, years, or—worse—your whole life, you know precisely how seductive a pedestal can be.

Finally, there is someone who is acting out your wildest dreams for you. From a standing start, he quickly says the kind of things you had always hoped to hear *(but wondered if you ever would)*. He is the ardent suitor who won't take *"no"* for an answer. He tells you that none of the women he knew can compare with you.

*Are you gratified?* You bet you are.

And yet, even then the warning signs are there. He falls in love so hard and so fast. His persistence is a touch obsessive. His references to the women in his past are, by implication, less than charitable.

But it is okay, isn't it? Because he understands that *you* are **different** and special.

Your relationship is different *(and special)*. So that makes it okay to throw yourself into coupledom at breakneck speed. Allegedly.

Actually, it's far from okay to throw yourself into a relationship and coupledom at breakneck speed. It's pure car crash. But let's face it; when someone is promising you the relationship of your dreams—or at least that's what you tell yourself—why delay gratification? *Why risk losing it by not responding swiftly and gratefully enough?*

When you are really hungry and someone puts a delectable dish of food in front of you, you don't sit and observe it cautiously for hours on end; you just pitch in. Is it too much of a stretch to say that you felt as if you were starving for an adoring lover?

It's not every day you get to be someone's dream woman, gazing down on more prosaic couples from the height of the pedestal on which he has placed you.

**Dream on!**

**Most of us tend to be seduced by the pedestal fantasy**. Why wouldn't we be? As I write this, I'm listening to some romantic pop lyrics: *"It feels like nobody ever loved me till you loved me."* Seductive, aren't they? Lyrics like this soothe the ear and addle the brain. They should probably come with a government health warning.

The truth about pedestals is, generally, far less glorious than the fantasy. A pedestal is a piece of furniture that is used to display something—or someone—to best advantage. There is, habitually, one pedestal per relationship. Mr Nasty carts his around with him as a vital part of his seduction kit. That way, he is ready when he meets a woman whom he thinks might be appropriate to park on it for a while.

The only thing is that he tends to be rather *"economical with the truth."* Does he tell *"his woman"* that she might as well enjoy the view from the pedestal while she is up there, because she won't be there for long?

Hardly.

He lulls her into a false sense of security—not hard because she is so invested in believing the fantasy.

Once she's well and truly hooked on the pedestal, of course, he starts to knock her off it. It was his pedestal, don't forget. He was the one who did the hard work of carting it around.

97

Heaven knows, **abusive men are not altruistic**. Whatever they do, they always do it with a view to their own gain.

**Abusive men subject their partners to *"pedestal training."*** This is essentially a three-stage process:

1. Accustom the woman to enjoy being put on a pedestal.
2. Habituate the woman to the idea of the pedestal being an integral part of the relationship.
3. Reclaim ownership of the pedestal and make it clear to the woman that her lot is to stand on the ground, looking up in deference at the rightful owner.

In other words, that pedestal is there for someone to be elevated on, certainly. But whatever the *short-term* arrangements, in the long term, the person standing on that pedestal is always going to be the abusive partner. That is how an abusive relationship works. Whether or not the abusive party was acting entirely consciously at the start does not much matter. The important thing is that his long-term agenda was always to hog that pedestal.

Sadly, you couldn't know that. You couldn't know that the tough experiences in your life left you horribly susceptible to the lure of the pedestal.

Fortunately, there is a valid alternative to the pedestal, and that's the slow burn. That is when a partner takes the *time* and *trouble* to love you for you, complete with all your vulnerabilities and foibles. **Time** and **trouble** are the key. He doesn't compare you, however favorably, to the *Other Women* in his life. That is just a way of saying that his feeling for you is better than a burnt stick in the eye. In the short term, anyway.

**Beware the pedestal**. It represents a real and present danger for you. You can expect to end up beneath it.

Know that in the topsy-turvy world of abuse, you will surely end up crushed by the combined, leaden weight of the pedestal and its owner.

# Abusive "Love" Is Rarely...

An e-mail landed in my inbox that crystalized the web of confusion that abusive partners spin around themselves. Here is how it read:

*Hi, Annie.*

*"I just read your article about recovering from an emotionally abusive relationship. I am in one right now and have been for almost two years. He is a very loving man and tells me all the time how beautiful I am and he always talks about marrying me and having children.*

*When he gets angry is when he starts bringing up things I've done in the past and makes me feel bad about myself. He gets angry if I imply he is controlling and says that he isn't. He professes and shows so much love to me, but he is also very emotionally abusive when he is angry or I do something he doesn't like. I basically live in isolation with no car or phone and I can't go anywhere without him. We share an e-mail address and I don't have my own Facebook page. He tells me I can do things but I don't, because I know that in reality it will make him upset. He doesn't insult my looks and he is completely dedicated to me, so is he still considered emotionally abusive?"*

There are **no prizes** for the correct answer.

Two things about this e-mail are interesting:

1.   The questioner clearly already knows the answer to her question. *But she is exercising a massive amount of denial.* She starts by stating—correctly—that she is in an abusive relationship. She ends by asking, *Is he still considered emotionally abusive if he says the right things and is "dedicated"?* I take "dedicated" to mean that he focuses a lot of his attention on her. Most likely he is obsessive, or *"all over her like a rash,"* rather than *devoted.*

2.   How the writer defines a *"loving"* man.

Some years ago now, I had my face read by face reader Glenna Trout. Glenna introduced me to the Three Rings of Relationships, and planted a comforting hand on my shoulder as she spoke of true intimacy *(the First Ring)* and the illusion of intimacy that occurs with Second Ringers. These are the people with whom you share an experience, an agenda, or a need.

Glenna's hand stayed planted firmly on my shoulder as two painful revelations sank in. The first was that my abusive husband had only ever been a Second Ringer,

101

whose need *(for a partner)* was, unfortunately, a good match for mine. The second revelation was even more painful: I had never experienced a true First Ring relationship.

Sadly, I don't think I was alone in this.

Abused women e-mail me all the time to talk about the love they share with an abusive, *loving* partner, and I find myself becoming increasingly crabby. Not with them, but with the persistence of the toxic notion that you can truly love someone and treat them badly.

Years ago, at a friend's wedding, I remember being rocked to the core when I first truly heard these words from Corinthians:

> *"Love is patient, Love is kind,*
> *It does not envy, it does not boast,*
> *It is not proud, it is not rude,*
> *It is not self-seeking,*
> *It is not easily angered,*
> *It keeps no record of wrongs.*
>
> *Love does not delight in evil,*
> *but rejoices with the truth.*
> *Love always protects, always trusts,*
> *always hopes, always perseveres.*
> *Love bears all things, believes all things,*
> *hopes all things, endures all things.*

*Love never ends.*
*Love never fails."*

*(1 Corinthians 13:4-8)*

That didn't sound too much like my abusive *"other half."* I don't suppose it sounds like yours either.

But suppose you were to write, instead, about abusive *"love."* That would read something like this:

> Abusive love is rarely patient,
> Abusive love is rarely kind,
> It does envy, it does boast,
> It is proud, it is rude,
> It is self-seeking,
> It is easily angered,
> It keeps a detailed record of wrongs.
> Abusive love delights in destruction,
>         but does not rejoice with the truth.
> Abusive love rarely protects, rarely trusts,
>         rarely hopes, rarely perseveres.
> Abusive love bears nothing, believes nothing,
>         hopes nothing, endures nothing.
> Abusive love soon ends.
> Abusive love fails.

Now *that* sounds just like my abusive ex-partner—and I'm guessing it sounds like yours also.

**When you said, *"I love you"* to your abusive partner,** you doubtless surrendered your heart and your independence.

When he said, *"I love you,"* he took possession of your heart and your independence.

What did he give in return?

The most charitable answer is that he gave as much as he was capable of giving—which, over time, was destined to embody the law of diminishing returns.

A more cynical, but probably accurate, answer is that he gave just as much as he needed to give in order to get what he wanted.

As to what he wanted, that was not *you*, but the use-value you represented.

If it had been *you* that he wanted, why would he have worked to deprive you of your freedom, your safety, your self-worth, your trust, your confidence, your dreams, and your vitality?

Why would he not have celebrated *you*?

And when will *you* start to celebrate you?

# Abusive "Love" Is...

There was a heartfelt response from a lot of readers to the previous article about abusive love. Clearly it resonated with them.

**We stay in an abusive relationship because we become Denial Superstars:** we manage **not** to see what is in front of our eyes.

Talking of which, a dear friend berated me for appealing primarily to other *"auditory"* people, like me. We auditory people are comfortable with words; we need them by the hundred—by the thousand is good too. But the more *"visual"* people struggle with large amounts of words. It has **nothing** to do with intelligence, and everything to do with the way the brain works.

Visual people see a great *"wodge"* of words and their brain can turn off—just as mine does when it comes to doing anything technical on the computer.

So, for once, I'm trying a far more *"visual"* approach. In this article, at least, I am using fewer words than usual and asking you to engage more actively.

When abused women talk about the love they have for their partner, they are, unwittingly, tapping into the reverence we all feel for *Love*. It jolts me every time.

**Abused women frequently tell me how *"loving"* their partner is**—at least when he is not living up to his Mr Nasty job description.

Abusive love, *if* there is such a thing, is a far cry from nurturing love.

To make the point, I rewrote the verses from Corinthians as they might look at an abuser's wedding. If, by any chance, he was playing fair, that revised version is how they might read.

That is, approximately, the relationship contract you *(and I)* signed up to. Had we only know that,

**Abusive love is rarely patient, Abusive love is rarely kind.**

*Would we have signed up to that contract knowingly?* Unlikely.

But we stay and we manage to find Mr Nasty *"lovable"* because we fixate on the contract he was not offering and we minimize his ill-treatment of us.

Here's an opportunity for you to be absolutely honest with yourself about how your abusive partner treated— or treats—you.

Simply answer all the questions that follow on a scale of 0–10. Zero means *not true at all.* 10 means either, *totally and utterly true,* or *all the time.*

## Question

Score 0–10

1. My abusive lover is rarely patient…..

2. My abusive lover is rarely kind…..

3. My abusive lover is jealous…..

4. My abusive lover is boastful…..

5. My abusive lover is self-important…..

6. My abusive lover is rude…..

7. My abusive lover is self-seeking…..

8. My abusive lover is easily angered…...

9.    My abusive lover keeps a detailed record of wrongs.....

10.   My abusive lover is destructive.....

11.   My abusive lover is not honest.....

12.   My abusive lover is not protective.....

13.   My abusive lover betrays trust.....

14.   My abusive lover is profoundly negative.....

15.   My abusive lover is quick to complain.....

16.   My abusive lover soon stopped valuing the relationship.....

17.   My abusive lover trashes the relationship.....

**Total.....**

Clearly, the higher the score, the more you need to take action now. Because *now* you can see it in front of you.

Not so?

# Breaking The Abusers' Code

This week, I was working with a woman who said, as abused women almost invariably say, *"How could he say such hurtful things to me?"*

Actually this is a very bad question—for a number of reasons. These include:

- He can say those things because **being hurtful is part of his job description**: abusive men say abusive things. Mr Nasty is not called Mr Nasty for nothing. Period.

- Who better than you for him to say them to? If he says them to his boss, or his co-workers, he is more likely to have comeback. If he says them to people on the street, they will most probably ignore him, hit him, or reply in kind. Do you get the picture?

- Mr Nasty says these things because hurting you serves a purpose for him.

**Abusive men need to exercise power and control** over the lives of their partners—and, most commonly, their children also. The best way they have found to do this is by saying hurtful things and by behaving in hurtful, destructive ways.

When you stand back to look at it, this is a continuation of playground behavior. It fits perfectly with the awareness that abusive behaviors are simply grown-up versions of toddlers' temper tantrums. These tantrums differ only in two ways:

1. The language and behaviors used are *superficially* more sophisticated.
2. The intention is to cause you as much pain as necessary to bring you back into line.

*"How could he say such hurtful things to me?"* **is a bad question**, because it only leads to you providing yourself with bad answers, such as:

- He doesn't love me enough to treat me better.
- He's acting like a jerk *(true, but not necessarily helpful since it leaves you feeling even more sorry for yourself)*.
- It must be my fault. Other men don't behave like that.

- If he can talk to me like that, that means I must be as awful as he says I am.

These answers propel you, at speed, into *"Poor Me!"* syndrome.

The correct answer to the question, *"How could he say such hurtful things to me?"* is this: he is feeling insecure and inadequate about something. An adult—*by which I mean somebody who is prepared to take responsibility for their own behavior*—would address that insecurity. Mr Nasty silences his own sense of inadequacy… by visiting it on his partner.

**It is a clear case of** *"Kick the Cat"* **syndrome**; he makes himself feel better by visiting his bad feelings on the person whom he sees as being weaker and more defenseless than he is.

No prizes for that behavior, huh?

That's the theory. But let's deconstruct a bit. Let's see how it works in practice.

| **He Says** | *He Means* |
|---|---|
| "You're stupid." | *"When I tell you that you lack intelligence, it makes me feel smarter."* |
| "You're ugly." | *"Telling you that you are ugly increases my sense of my worth in the relationship."* |
| "You're fat." | *"Being critical of your body makes me feel more attractive."* |
| "You're selfish." | *"Don't tell me that you actually dare to have any needs, wants, dreams and desires of your own! Your sole role is to serve me unconditionally."* |
| "You're not feminine." | *"You aren't behaving like the totally subservient woman of my fantasy."* |
| "You are unloving." | *"You dared to express something other than unconditional adoration of* **me***!"* |
| "You act/think like a man." | *"How dare you have your own thoughts and opinions! You are meant to be my creature, my puppet."* |
| "You don't understand me." | *"You should be endlessly compassionate. Things are so hard for me."* |

112

| **He Says** | **He Means** |
| --- | --- |
| "You're not supportive." | *"You are not 150% supportive of me... even when I am clearly wrong."* |
| "You're a lousy mother." | *"I'm casting around for the single most hurtful thing I can say to wound you."* |
| "You don't do X, Y, and Z for me." | *"I want much, much more. I want all of your attention, your time, your energy, and your life's blood."* |
| "Nobody else would want you." | *"She's looking angry. I'd better remind her that she has nowhere else she could possibly go, or she might just leave me. That would be a terrible nuisance."* |
| "I'm leaving." | *"You're not paying enough attention to me. A good threat will focus your mind nicely."* |

There are other favorite, time-honored code phrases of abusive men, also. All of them are, actually, about him, *not about you.*

You have never understood them because *you* entered into a contract to love, and be loved by, this man.

He entered into a contract that, had it worked out in accordance with his most cherished fantasy, would have given him a:

- Barbie Doll
- Cheerleader
- Earth Mother
- Superwoman
- Porn star
- Slave
- Guardian angel
- Cook, cleaner, and general dogs-body
- Strong woman

And much, much more.

How strange that reality did not pan out like his fantasy!

However, the upside for him is that, although he didn't get lucky *(there's a surprise!)*, he did get someone he could abuse and humiliate whenever the need or the fancy took him. *(And he had already sussed that out from very early on.)* So *he* didn't lose out.

The bottom line is this: **His ill-treatment of you is not a reflection on you**; it's all about him. That is what he needs in order to feel halfway good about himself. *(Halfway good is about the best he can ever hope for.)*

Knowing all this, you don't have to be hurt when he resorts to The Abusers' Code.

He's just reminding you that the two of you don't speak the same language. **You speak *"Love"*… he speaks *"Hurt."***

Yes, he can *"get by"* in *"Love"* when he needs to. But it is not his native language, not a language he enjoys speaking or in which he can express himself fully.

Leave him to his language—and put yourself out of his misery.

# "A Broken Wing"

Today I had the feeling that I must have been living on the moon for years.

Why?

Because I *finally* discovered Martina McBride's *"A Broken Wing." (For anyone else who has been living on the moon, you can listen to this wonderful anthem on Youtube.)* The lyrics left me absolutely speechless. You could not find a more perfect way to sum up the reality of living in an abusive relationship:

> *"She loved him like he was*
> *The last man on earth.*
> *Gave him everything she ever had.*
> *He'd break her spirit down,*
> *Then come lovin' up on her.*
> *Give a little then take it back.*
> *She'd tell him 'bout her dreams,*
> *He'd just shoot 'em down.*

*Lord he loved to make her cry..."*

Sure, the accompanying video is a little sanitized—the big house, the glossy lifestyle *(even the "designer lettuce")*, with the violence just implied. But anyone who has been there can easily flesh out that outline!

So why is it so important to me right now?

Because of my own healing journey. That is exactly the way it was for me—although I could never have conveyed the essence so powerfully and economically. Like the women I work with, I have had to work through the various staging posts along that journey.

- **First, you have to understand** that the treatment you have received has been **deliberate**. It really was designed to *"break your spirit down,"* break your wings and make you emotionally dependent on your captor. Boy, does it work! *(Not a week goes by without a number of women e-mailing me to tell me they can't stop loving a man who treats them badly.)*

- So **you learn that there are lots of dangerous men out there**—dangerous men who can sense a vulnerable woman across half a county, and home in mercilessly on their prey.

- **You learn to keep well away from them** *(and, quite possibly, **all** men)* while you rebuild your self-worth and keep yourself safe.

- **You learn to trust yourself,** so that you can start to extend your trust, *where appropriate*, to other people.

- **You learn that people have to earn your trust,** by behaving in a way that does not jar with your **intuition**. Anyone who has ever lived with an abuser knows that, if you listen to their words, they can persuade you that they have every right to cast the first stone, and as many others as they might feel like, at you. They will persuade you that night is day, and that you are the worst person in the world while they are the best. They do this despite their own possible addictions, and any number of behaviors that society condemns, including being utterly two-faced, and treating you like dirt. *(Your conscious mind can be persuaded to believe pretty much anything with enough brainwashing. Your intuition can be silenced, but it can never be persuaded. Intuition is not much given to repeating itself, so when it speaks, however softly, you would do well to trust it and listen.)*

- **You learn, as you heal, that a lot of your fear is leftover fear**. It relates to events in the past, and yet you carry it into the present.

- **You learn to trust yourself** to bring your new knowledge, courage, and self-worth to a new relationship. You come to trust that you will **not** dissolve into the small, terrified, hopeless puddle of a woman you once were. That is a pretty serious concern, and, by the time you start to voice it, you have already put a lot of distance between you and that abused woman, or you could not even think that way. Still, it is a legitimate concern. Having been so profoundly disempowered, it is only sane to be wary of the possibility of ever allowing it to happen again.

- **You learn that X means X, not Y, or Z**. Everyone learns to make sense of the world, for themselves, as children. As we well know, children are, sadly, in many ways defenseless, and so they make it their business to learn fast. Swift learning is the best way to protect themselves from pain. So they generalize from a specific situation. Like my client who had *"learned"* that she was hopeless with numbers because a math teacher had said so when she was nine. Abused women learn that men are dangerous, that intimacy is destructive. They still have a mental *"map of the world"* in which all relationships are

119

*bound to be* the same as an abusive relationship. Some women shy away from relationships; others rush into physical intimacy. Both tendencies are, I believe, attempts to avoid the risk of exposing their spirit to the vulnerability of intimacy.

- **You learn that good men, and good people, behave in caring ways.** The time comes when you finally see the gulf that divides abusive men from good men, and abusive relationships from good relationships. Bad behaviors are most commonly the sign of a bad man and a bad relationship. At the very least, they are the sign of someone you would do well to steer clear of until such time as they have sorted out their own life.

- **You learn that if a man acts like a small child having a temper tantrum,** he probably **is** a small child who has temper tantrums. That may be a job for *"Supernanny"*; it certainly isn't a role for *an equal partner.*

- **You learn that, if abuse is a downward spiral, healing is an upward spiral.**

- **You learn that true intimacy nurtures; it does not harm.**

- You learn that your once broken wing will not stop you from flying.

# "Did I Really Deserve Abuse?"

I received an e-mail that ended with the words that follow:

> *"I do recognize my codependency traits and low self-esteem issues which made me opt for a bad relationship with this man, but DID I REALLY DESERVE ABUSE? WAS I ENTIRELY RESPONSIBLE? Kindly help me face these demons of my past."*

I don't remember anyone ever posing the question quite as succinctly before.

The answer is twofold.

The first part is that the sum of your past life experiences and expectations may well leave you **open to abuse**.

To put it another way, if you have grown up in an abusive home environment, then you are **already programmed for abuse**. It is what you know.

122

By the same token, if you are currently reeling from some experience that has left you at rock bottom, then you are susceptible to abusive programming.

So, the first part of the answer is that women who find themselves in an abusive relationship do so because **circumstances** have laid them **open to abuse**.

Being open—in the sense of being vulnerable—to abuse comes about simply as an unfortunate conjunction of circumstances. However, that does not, in any way, justify abuse.

**Nobody ever deserves to be abused. Ever.**

In reality, **abuse speaks volumes about the abuser**, far more so than it does about the person abused.

It tells you the abuser feels he has an absolute right to visit his fury and destructive feelings on another person. It tells you that, at bottom, Mr Nasty feels as worthless and unlovable and needy as he tells you that you are. It tells you that, fundamentally, he really cannot bear himself.

*(And, honestly, who could possibly blame him for feeling like that...* **about himself?!***)*

The second part of the answer may be less obvious.

**We receive what we believe we deserve.**

Now, this is not the belief that you or I grew up with. Most likely, you grew up with the notion that, if you were a very good girl, good things would happen to you. The corollary of that was that if you did not match up to a *(self-appointed)* arbiter's notion of *"good behavior,"* then, as surely as night follows day, less nice things would happen to you.

They did, of course. Because that arbiter of *"deservingness"* was also the **enforcer** of consequences.

Most of us, including me, grew up nicely programmed to expect, **and accept**, that our failings, mistakes and limitations would result in consequences that we would not relish. And they did.

We are not talking morality here; we are not talking about actions that would be harmful to society, but simply actions that are offensive to the arbiter of *"deservingness,"* because they do not conform to his agenda. *(Have you ever been punished by your abusive partner because you forgot to tiptoe around sufficiently when he was "tired"?)*

Be honest with yourself: you don't really believe that you deserve very much, do you? You probably know, with your head, that you deserve happiness, and  other good things. But my guess is you don't believe it with your heart.

If you believed with your heart that you were deserving of the best that life and love have to offer, there is no way that you would stick with a partner who treats you with the lack of care and respect that you endure. *(The same lack of care and respect that I endured, and every other abused woman endures.)*

If you believed with your heart that you were deserving of good things, you would, at the very least, be long gone.

More correctly, you would never even have got yourself into that abusive relationship in the first place. Because there was a point at the very start when you knew the man was not worthy of you... And yet, at some point, the belief that you deserved so little that you would have to settle for what was on offer kicked in.

So here is a thought for you: **You are deserving**. You exist; that is enough to guarantee your deserving status.

You see, your deservingness does not detract from the deservingness of any other being on the planet. It is not as if there is only a fixed, non-renewable amount of deservingness, and when you take from it a share, however small, you deprive another person. That is not how it works—at all.

Rather, your failure to own your deservingness impoverishes others. Because it is only when you truly own something that you can generate it for the people around you. Especially the people you love.

When you feel truly deserving of receiving good things, not only do you automatically safeguard yourself from abusers—because why would you, *willingly*, swallow their poison?—but you show others how possible it is for them to step into deservingness also.

So, **when are you going to step up to the plate** and make the decision to own your deservingness?

You never deserved abuse and owning your deservingness does not need to be anywhere near as challenging as it may sound to you. What really stands in the way of your healing is not a lack of self-worth but a lack of knowledge. The thing that you need, in order to move forward, is not a *"positive beliefs transplant" (such things never work)* but a simple roadmap that you can follow.

Instead of wasting your time and energy asking the dreaded questions, *"Did I really deserve abuse? Was I responsible?"* that keep you focused on your past and your pain, focus on all the things that will help you to move from where you are now to the life that you want for yourself.

# In Praise of Abused Women

Let's face it; we live in a culture that feels uncomfortable around victims. The Brits, especially, love an underdog *(who, by definition, fights back despite their weakness)*. We show compassion towards suffering, and persecuted groups. But individual victims make us feel defensive. Abused women are, obviously, prime illustrations of this group. It's easy to blame them for their misfortune.

I remember watching *Sleeping with the Enemy*, in which Julia Roberts stars as the battered wife who fakes her own death in order to escape her gilded hell. And I remember thinking,

> *"How could she have got herself into that mess?"*

Even as I sat next to my own emotionally abusive partner, I managed to be unaware that I lived with the same kind of fear and misery. *(Denial truly does catapult you into a topsy-turvy world!)*

127

Once you start to move away from an abusive relationship, you feel obliged to blame yourself for your stupidity, for not knowing better. This self-flagellation may be a first step on the journey to recovery but, equally, it is a way in which you—unintentionally—revisit abusive judgments on yourself.

Recovery requires self-discovery. It obliges us to own responsibility for our lack of boundaries and self-love, our failure, and our naïve view of the *"power of love."* It also obliges us—and rightly so—to make a strong commitment to ourselves.

Healing requires that we learn to love ourselves. Why should we not learn to celebrate the special qualities that we bring to our relationships?

I am reminded at this point of the quotation that there are no weaknesses, only overdone strengths. Abused women overdo generosity, selflessness, devotion, trust, and faith to name but a few.

There is another one that has struck me very forcefully of late. We are visionaries; we hold a vision of what our partner *could* be—in the best of all possible worlds.

In my coaching practice, I work a lot with the power of positive expectation. Part of my role is to hold a vision for my clients until they can hold it for themselves. In most contexts, that is a very powerful tool for healing.

So why does it not work with an abusive partner?

First, as a coach, I hold that vision, but the client does her own work. Whereas as a wife, I was prepared to shoulder my husband's emotional burden *and* do all the work for him. Just like any other abused woman does.

Second—and this is a powerful thought to take on board—an abusive man has no real wish to change; his psychopathology may well mean that he can't anyway. In other words, *you are flogging a dead horse*—your effort is utterly misplaced.

One of the things people don't tell you, unfortunately, is that not all relationships are created equal.

Still, discovering that *he* cannot change is very freeing. Because, unlike him, you still have that wonderful gift of being able to hold a healing expectation. If you could do it for another person who put you down mercilessly, then you can certainly learn to do it for yourself. My book *"The Woman You Want To Be"* is specially designed to walk women who feel anything but positive through the process of creating—and getting comfortable with— positive expectations about what is possible for them.

Sure, you have learnt from a master how to feel terrible about yourself, and you are nearly as effective at putting yourself down as he ever was, but that is as nothing compared with your dogged determination.

You really are allowed to offer yourself as much love, support and belief as you ever offered your partner. You are allowed to hold a vision, *for yourself also*, of all that is great about you—in ways you may not even begin to suspect yet.

Why not give it a go? And remember, that means committing to that vision over the months and years. *(Sure, you will experience "wobbles" of self-doubt along the way but that just proves you are human. You can acknowledge the "wobble" and then refocus on that positive vision.)*

After all, you held positive expectations for someone who didn't thank you for it, and whose life you could never change. If you could do that for an emotionally abusive partner, why not do it now for the one person whose life you *do* have the power to transform?

# Lies Abused Women Tell Themselves

**There are, apparently, two kinds of abused women:** those who grow up in a climate of abuse and those who grow up in functional families, enjoy a healthy relationship but then become vulnerable either through bereavement or another major life crisis.

Of the many, many women who have spoken or written to me over the years, offhand I can only think of two who belong to the second category.

However different their past experiences of relationships may have been, though, in the course of their abusive relationship the beliefs of these two groups of women become tragically indistinguishable.

This happens because abused women try very hard to learn from their relationships. They are desperate to learn what they are doing wrong so that they can change it.

There are, essentially, two ways that they learn. The first is from what their partner says. The second is from **their interpretation** of his behavior.

**An abusive partner rapidly becomes the most influential person** in your life.

He has the power to take you to dizzy heights of happiness. *(However, the statistical odds of this happening decrease markedly the longer the relationship limps on.)*

He has the power to plunge you into the depths of despair, and usually does. When he does, as his partner you feel the need to explain to yourself what has happened. After all, you have been consistently programmed to believe that Mr Nasty is a precious diamond *(albeit a diamond in the rough)*. Therefore the problems in the relationship cannot really be his. That being the case, they must be *yours*—right?

Theoretically, there is good news here: if the responsibility for what goes wrong with the relationship lies with you, then you have only to discover what you are doing wrong to be able to change it. Then Mr Nasty will shed the harshness he sometimes exhibits and forever after you and he will live a life of unparalleled joy and delight...

*(Only that just doesn't work, because Mr Nasty has **no interest** in the relationship changing. Why should he have? He has you as his scapegoat.)*

Derren Brown, the wonderful illusionist and mentalist specializes in exposing how susceptible human beings are to superstition. Recently, I watched him create a situation that encouraged five people, of proven intelligence, to believe that their random, meaningless acts could produce the outcome they desired.

The best of it was that these five resourceful individuals became so obsessed with futile behaviors and looking for futile meanings, that they missed the solution which he had displayed, quite prominently, hidden in full view—had they only had the mindfulness to look. Only they did not look.

My guess is that you have probably done the same in your relationship. I know I did.

So, here are some of the lies that blind abused women to the reality of their relationship that is hidden in full view.

**"It's all my fault."** Is your partner perhaps a newborn baby who can avoid all responsibility for his own behavior? When Mr Nasty screams obscenities, foams at the mouth, punches holes in the wall, or worse, does he have absolutely no control? *Are you really that powerful? (If so, how come you generally feel so powerless in the situation?)*

**"I'm being stupid."** Yes, you are—but not for the reasons you think. If you can totally discount your profound feelings of unhappiness, then that *is* a kind of emotional stupidity—and something that I have been guilty of also. If you are unhappy around Mr Nasty, the message you need to hear is that being around him makes you miserable. You can be much happier without him—once you get over the belief that you need him to make you happy.

**"He doesn't mean it/doesn't want to hurt me."** Maybe, just maybe, if he had only ever said the hurtful things once, that might be true. But when they become a regular part of his repertoire, you'd better believe that either:

  a)  Mr Nasty doesn't care what he says to exert control over you, or
  b)  He means them.

**"He's had a hard time."** Okay, so that one may be true. The thing is, so have you. And you're putting all your energies into trying to make his life sweeter. This means that you have taken the decision to create something meaningful precisely *because* of your past unhappiness. Sure, it will be even better when you start focusing on doing it for yourself rather than another wounded soldier. But if you are capable of making that choice, how come he isn't?

**"I just know we can be happy together."** Funny then, isn't it, that you are saying this at a time when you feel as low as you have ever felt in your whole life, and he has a lot to do with it? Given half a chance, I know, you will tell me how happy you were at the beginning. *(If I had a dime for every time I've heard that story, I would be living in a palazzo in Venice, looking out at the gondolas gliding up and down the Grand Canal.)*

But here's the thing: your happiness spiel is the expurgated version. Behind it lies a less attractive tale about the things that worried you about Mr Nasty from the word *go*. That is, before he set to work hypnotizing you with his silver-tongued lies about knowing that you were so wonderful you could make his life perfect. *(Now, **there's** a tall order. If he can't be bothered to do the work of doing what it takes to improve his own life for himself, it's just not going to happen. That's an unspoken law of the universe.)*

**"He has so much potential."** Maybe he has and maybe he hasn't. You are not his teacher, his boss, or his agent. Still less are you his parent or his psychotherapist. Unless he is under the age of about 16—and I sincerely hope he is not—realizing *his* potential is his responsibility. Besides, I don't really think you are talking about his potential to succeed in the world. What you are concerned with is Mr Nasty's potential to become a great life partner. Since he reckons you are lucky to have him—temper tantrums and all—he clearly does not share your concern.

135

**"I'm ruining/have ruined the best relationship I can ever expect."** There are two glaring inaccuracies in this brief phrase. First, *the best relationship?* Yes, you may have had some other dire relationships, but you wouldn't be in a state of emotional meltdown now if this was a good relationship. *You would be happy, relaxed, and confident.*

Everything about it screams **'bad relationship'**—and you know it. As for it being the best you can ever expect, that's what he has told you, isn't it? So it must be right. Because abusive men are never wrong. Ever. Are they? About anything. Sure, some present themselves very credibly to the outside world, but you know as well as I do that within the confines of their home they have a pretty skewed view about most things.

**"It's not him, it's me."** Well, at least the two of you agree on something: your hopelessness. It *can* be the basis for a relationship, as you have already discovered. But it's certainly not the basis for a happy, functional one.

These are not the only lies that abused women tell themselves, but they are some of the key destructive ones. If they are lies that *you* have been telling yourself, the time has come to think seriously, now, about getting out. Your relationship is a sow's ear; it's never going to be a silk purse. More to the point, your partner may be a frog, but he will never be a prince.

You, on the other hand, have so many generous and loving qualities. They are what took you into this relationship in the first place. They are still with you. It's time you thought seriously about getting out and lavishing some of your love on *yourself*. You will be amazed how rich the rewards will be.

# Better To Have Somebody Than Nobody?

**Why do we stay with Mr Nasty?**
Here are some of the reasons that I hear most
commonly from women,

- "I can't manage financially without him."
- "It's better for the kids to have two parents."
- "I still love him."
- "I'll never get anyone else as good again."
- "It's better to have someone than nobody."

Do you notice a common thread in those arguments?
Apart from the fact that you, too, have probably said all
of those things at some point.

They are all statements of low self-worth. The common
thread is a lack of trust in yourself, and in your own
resources.

**"I can't manage financially without him"** may be an
accurate statement right now, but it can always change.

Many, many women lack the energy to earn a living when they are with an abusive man; that goes with the territory. An abusive relationship is an exhausting business. However, these same women suddenly discover their personal power and monetize their skills, once they are free from the drain on their emotional strength.

**"It's better for the kids to have two parents."** There are a number of variants on this, including, *"He may be a pig as a partner, but he's a good dad."* While this is possible, it's highly unlikely. If a partner will abuse you emotionally, and maybe physically as well, either in front of or under the same roof as his children, he is not such a great dad. His behavior will, inevitably, damage those children. They grow up with the deplorable model of an abusive relationship in front of their eyes. **Children learn from their parents' reality**. In time, they will surely replicate it. Telling them not to make your mistakes will not change that.

**"I still love him."** This one kills me these days. Not that I haven't said it myself. I *"loved"* my abusive husband, as much as any abused woman loves her abuser. I wanted the best for him. I wanted his return to emotional well-being. *(He had to be unhappy or he wouldn't behave like that, I rationalized.)* Above all, I wanted to turn back time so he could revert to being the lover I still remembered—through heavily rose-tinted glasses—from the early days.

What I really wanted was to import that long gone past into the future.

Of course, I didn't ask myself too often what I loved about him. Better not to. The essence of the man, in my humble opinion, was pretty good. Potential never dies, I believed. It was just his behaviors that were inexcusable.

How does that one work? How can we swallow our own propaganda that we love the man, when we loathe the way he behaves?

**"I'll never find anyone as good again."** Think about it for a moment: can an abusive man ever really be described as good? Still we obsess about his—alleged—good qualities, and/or the good parts of the relationship.

If your abusive relationship were a car, it would be an old, *un*-roadworthy Smart for two, or a Fiat 500. You would look at it and say, *"Well, it has a steering wheel, and a chassis, and lights, and wing mirrors."* Then you would tell yourself that it was similar enough to the Rolls Royce you really want.

**No, it is not!**

You wouldn't let somebody sell you a car that was way below the specification you were paying for. But that is exactly what you do in an abusive relationship; you settle for a vehicle with neither engine, nor wheels, that will never, ever take you where you want to go.

**"It's better to have somebody than nobody."**

*Where, oh where, did we women learn that one?*

If you think back a hundred years ago, that may have been true. It certainly is not now.

Besides, **in an abusive relationship, you *don't* have somebody**.

Yes, there is a living, breathing person erupting *(I use the term advisedly)* in your life. But this is someone who, as often as not, makes it very clear to you that they really, really do not like, respect, or value you.

*(Wo)manfully* overlooking this important consideration, you attempt to share your innermost feelings, your body, and your life with such a person.

And that leads to profound loneliness.

You don't need me to tell you about the loneliness of an abusive relationship. It is probably the most agonizing loneliness you will ever feel. It is the pain of something that we do not have, and very probably never had, like the pain of an amputated limb.

Being alone, and **free** to connect with your thoughts, feelings, passions, and hopes, your past, present and future, your friends and family will never be half as lonely as the loneliness of your empty relationship. Your aloneness is a state you are free to fill however you choose.

Your abusive relationship, on the other hand, is a state of solitary confinement, over which you have no control...

So, is it better to have somebody than nobody?

Yes, it is. But that somebody will **never** be your abusive partner.

**Mr Nasty is not yours to have and enjoy.**

He never was. An abusive man is not unlike a slot machine; every once in a while you may hit the jackpot.

*But in the end you get about as much care and affection from an abusive man as you would from that slot machine.*

It is all about the somebody.

The somebody that you *can* have is, of course, yourself.

The chances of loving and valuing yourself while you stay with an abuser are minimal. But leave and you can

142

soon learn to redirect that river of love and nurturing from your abusive partner to yourself. He never appreciated it, because it was not what he was looking for.

He had a talent for mistaking diamonds for dross.

When you hold those stones in your own hand and look at them through your own eyes, you will see that they are diamonds.

Your life and your love are precious. Don't lavish them on somebody who will only ever throw them back in your face.

# The "Joys" Of Being A Victim

Recently, I found myself wallowing in a sense of grievance; a woman I had known for some time was judging me, and she found me wanting. But how could she judge me? She'd never know how hard it had been for me... *blah, blah, blah*. She had not had to... *blah, blah, blah*. You can probably finish those statements as well as I can.

There was a weird kind of coziness about my feelings. I was right back in the old victim mindset; a familiar sense of hopelessness was taking over...

It was at this point that I phoned Shoshana, a dear friend who is no stranger to these feelings herself. We talked briefly about feelings of victimhood and how powerful they are.

I asked her, **"What benefits does feeling like a victim give us?"** Her knee-jerk reaction was to say, *"None."* We agreed that it saps our energy, our feelings of self-worth, our hope, our sense of meaning. And yet...

We decided to stay with it and look at the payoffs. What follows is the list that came up and held true for both of us.

Now, you may be different and, if you are, I take my hat off to you. If you recognize yourself in the list that follows, that is great too. These are not pretty things to have to admit to, but you are in good company. Quite literally *millions* of other women will see their own reflections in this list.

Besides, once the list is out in the open, it enables you to put a different perspective on those feelings.

By the time Shoshana and I had finished compiling the list, we were shrieking with laughter. Not because our experiences were funny; that kind of experience is never funny. Not because we deserved to be laughing stocks; we – and our experiences - are always worthy of respect. But the position that Shoshana and I had staked out for ourselves was so unproductive as to be funny.

The reason why a person resorts to *"victimhood"* is never funny. Between having a victim identity or no identity, the victim identity has to be preferable. But it is always the corner into which you have been pushed. Before you can move out of that corner—and stay out of that corner—you need to recognize when you are in the *"corner mindset."*

In the end the choice is simple: you cannot go back and rewrite your history, so there is nothing to be gained by wishing that you could. **You can be wronged, or you can move forward**. And, of course, you will have to remake your choice repeatedly.

**Which will you choose**: the joys of victimhood, or the rich rewards of having a joyful life?

To help you avoid the all-too-normal temptation to wallow, what follows is a *brief* list of the joys of victimhood.

- **Being *"different"***—*"I'm not the same as other people because I am going through so much more sh\*te."* Being different lends itself to the *"Yes, but…"* syndrome: *"Because I'm different, nothing you say applies to me. My suffering sets me apart."*

- ***Being "special"***—*"Other people don't have the same intensity of emotion [read **misery**] that I do. This makes me special."*

- **Having it harder than other people.** Well, you have, haven't you? It's not easy to look around and see other people who have some support or saving grace that you don't have. Whether or not this belief is true, *is it useful? How does holding this belief help you to move your life forward?*

- **Taking the moral high ground,** on account of another person's appalling treatment of you. *(Sure, it's pretty lonely and cold up there but, still, it feels better than being down in the mud where he kept you. Actually, there are other places. There are hillsides, seasides, villages. Create a vision and you can start to move towards it.)*

- **You have a dramatic story to tell.** This does two things: it commands attention—and respect—and it establishes status and identity. You are a person who has been through so many awful things. One way or another, people have to acknowledge that. In reality, some will, and some will decide they can't hack it after a while; that is another injustice you suffer.

- **You get to abdicate responsibility.** Certainly you did not cause the toxic relationship in your life. Your abusive partner has his own responsibility for that. Nevertheless, you did, at some level, attract and allow an abusive relationship to happen to you. Every abused woman I have ever worked with had an intuition at the start of the relationship. She sensed that she was making a mistake and she overrode that intuition. Accepting responsibility does **not** mean

147

shouldering blame; the two things are quite separate. But what you do not own, you cannot change. Responsibility makes you the creator of your life, which means that you can make different choices in the future with different results. Victimhood leaves you stuck.

- **You get to escape change.** Going round and round the closed circuit of your story again and again means that you have no energy and no opening for change. Because he has told you endlessly how much harder life will be without him, you end up believing that *"different"* means *"worse."* (*Although, when you stop to think about it, he wasn't usually either that truthful or accurate in his predictions.*)

- **You get to keep thinking small.** This one comes up again and again in my workshops. There comes a point when women can embrace a new way of thinking, with new insights, new visions and new hope; or they can stick with the known. You can't do both at the same time. Some women see the big picture and go straight for it. A few prefer to stay with the small, known picture. They might say, *"When the mess I am in is over, then I will think bigger."* But for as long as they focus on the mess, that mess will dominate their consciousness.

- **You avoid the challenge of feeling happy in the moment.** I've heard the argument that *"being happy just sets you up for disappointment"* about as often as I've had hot dinners lately. I don't buy it. Expecting disappointment sets you up for disappointment. Being happy in the moment teaches you to be happy in the moment. I'm guessing that even if you can't eat in a 5-star restaurant every night, you will still eat on a daily basis, and quite often enjoy what you eat. The same goes for happiness; why not enjoy whatever you can get now? It beats *un*happiness. It really doesn't take much enjoyment of the moment to make a dent in profound feelings of unhappiness.

- **You're able to totally avoid having fun!**

- **You don't have to be positive, ever.**

- **You don't have to love yourself *at all*.** You can be at least as hard on yourself as Mr Nasty ever was.

Victims focus on loss and lack. In most cases, they have been programmed by an abusive partner to focus on loss and lack.

What do you lose when you step out of that mindset? **Absolutely nothing.**

How do you get out of it? Understanding about abuse will inform you, but it won't necessarily set you free. You get out of it by starting to focus on yourself in a caring, positive way.

Now, I'm aware that you may well not know how to do this for yourself. And why don't you know how to do this for yourself? *Because nobody ever taught you.* Most people don't know *how* to teach you. Either people were lucky and were born into a nurturing, supportive family—in which case loving themselves came naturally to them—or else the concept is totally alien to them.

Happily, you can *learn* to love yourself. You can start anytime you choose. It may take a little while, but it is very doable. It **will** work.

Victimhood has its own small rewards. There are much bigger ones out there waiting for you. You just have to **make the decision** to step out of that small, claustrophobic circle of misery.

# "It's Not About You!"

When you are in an abusive relationship, you quickly discover that everything you do is wrong.

The message Mr Nasty gives you loud and clear is that it's all about you and what you do wrong.

The relationship can't work *because of what you do wrong*. He loses his temper sometimes and becomes hostile *because of what you do wrong*. If he doesn't have a job, that is *because of what you do wrong*. If he has a job and is desperately unhappy then that's *because of what you do wrong*. Everything bad that happens in his life is somehow *because of what you do wrong*.

If something good were to happen, which it rarely does, that would not be about you; that would be about him. And if, by chance, it *does* happen, life will surely fall back into the old negative default pattern before long, and that will be *because of what you do wrong*.

A crude, but accurate, rule of thumb would be this: Everything is always entirely your fault, *because of what you do wrong.*

It's not surprising abused women think that *"It"* is all about them. They hear that often enough.

But here's the curious thing: **abusive men all say much the same thing, the world over.** *(And, as a result, abused women all believe much the same thing about themselves.)*

Now, I'm not a great believer in coincidence at the best of times, and in this case I don't buy it for a moment. When you find abusive men, rich and poor, thousands and thousands of miles apart, coming out with the same negative claptrap, that is never coincidence. That is programming.

How does it happen?

As I see it, when people refuse to take responsibility for themselves, they end up acting out some primitive programming.

What do I mean by that?

Think back either to your own playground days, or your children's. Say a small child falls over, or experiences some other kind of mishap. How often does he or she explain it by saying, *"X pushed me!"* or, *"Y made me...'*?

152

As small children see it something bad happens to them, through no fault of their own, through the malevolence of someone or something. The bad thing has nothing whatsoever to do with them, it merely befalls them.

**An essential part of growing up consists of learning to take**—*appropriate*—**responsibility for ourselves and our actions**. That may not always be enjoyable but it is what adults do. Unfortunately, it's something abusive men choose **not** to learn in their intimate relationships. I say *"choose"* because some abusive men behave horribly badly in their intimate relationships yet, choose to act responsibly in the outside world.

Why would these men make different choices in the outside world to those they make in their own home? Because they have a shrewd idea of what they need to do to get by in each environment.

When an abusive man chose you, he had already sounded out your capacity for compliance and, at the very least, he *knew* that you would accept his worldview. It may have been *"the two of you against the world"* at the start, but the key word in that was **against**; not *"two,"* as you probably hoped and believed.

**Abusive men are still playing out the small child's view of the world**, in which they are the center of everything. If a situation pans out differently, if they are *denied* their place at the center of your universe, they will throw a temper tantrum to re-establish their desired status quo. *(When have you known an abusive man genuinely negotiate and defer to his partner?)*

An abuser's **temper tantrums are never about you.** He chose you because he wanted someone who would make him right and reflect an idealized view of him back to him.

You wanted someone who, in return for your love, would love, respect and care for you.

Ultimately, your Mr Nasty wanted someone who, in exchange for being *told* she was loved, would love, respect and care for him unconditionally. He might have been prepared to mouth the right words to you, but he was never going to **show** love, respect and care in his behavior towards you—or any other woman.

You were prepared to show love, through considerate actions; he was not.

Abusive men may profess love for their partner but they do so without  showing true care or consideration.

Why?

**Because the relationship was never meant to be about you.**

The relationship exists simply so that they can fuel their need for a curious fusion of a *mother, status symbol, and whipping boy*. That's what they want and need.

You, as a person, were never terribly important in the relationship. In fact, the longer the relationship goes on the less important you become. In the end, you are meant to serve a purpose—like drugs or alcohol—to be used, or abused, to *maybe* dull his bad feelings and make him feel better about himself.

That doesn't work, of course.

Because only he can address his bad feelings, as only you can address yours.

If you are reading this today because you want to shed the trauma of an abusive relationship and you take only one thing from this piece, please, please, take this: **The relationship was never about you.**

The verbal, emotional, and physical punishment an abuser metes out always comes in a package with your name on. But it is never about you. It is simply toddler stuff delivered by a chronological adult.

Still don't believe me?

Just tune out from the words and observe the actions and the facial expressions. Whether that man is 17, 37,

77, or any age in between, he is having a temper tantrum. That temper tantrum is about not getting exactly what he wants precisely when he wants it; it is not about you.

# It's Not About You!—Part 2

I attended a weekend workshop run by a man who is a world leader in his field. It turns out that he is of a similar age, similar ethnicity, and has a similar background to my abusive ex-husband. He also exhibited similar behaviors and even had the same kind of coloring and build.

What does that tell me?

What it tells *me* is simply that they both had the same kinds of issues to deal with, and both preferred to visit their anger on others, rather than work through those issues.

Now, it probably won't surprise you to know that I did not warm excessively to this man. Still, his workshop delivered the value it offered. It also delivered a value I had not expected, which I believe is important enough to share with you.

This man spent most of the workshop being relentlessly upbeat. On the last day he shared with us the story of the worst time of his life, a time when he spiraled into despair and suicidal thoughts.

He was in that state of desperation when he bumped into a friend. This friend quickly summed up the situation. He knew that he had only a tiny window of opportunity; either he would reach the man with his words, or the man might well take his own life.

This is approximately what his friend said to him:

**"It's not about you! You have a mission. When you are a victim, you are just thinking about you. However, you are the only person who can live your mission, and if you don't do your mission, it won't get done. You are the only** *(and here he supplied the man's name)* **on earth."**

Now, that applies equally to you, too.

**I believe that you have a mission.** You are the only person on earth who can live that mission. I don't know what that mission is, and maybe you don't yet. But you will. And maybe all that you have been through in your abusive relationship is tempering you for that mission, so that you become stronger and clearer and wiser and more able to fulfill it.

158

Your mission is not about your story, in the sense that it is not about continuing to focus on the sadness of what you have been through, and lost. It's not about the fear and the pain you have experienced. That has certainly happened, and it is right for you to honor that.

You need to turn more of your attention to your mission—whether that mission lies in giving your child/children a better chance than you had, or creating something that you hardly dare to entertain in your mind right now.

You have a mission that only you can fulfill. Whether or not you know what that mission is right now is immaterial. When the time is right that knowledge will become apparent to you. Meanwhile, let the thought that you have a unique mission that only you can fulfil sustain you, even as your abusive partner or ex-partner continues to drone on—either outside or *inside* your head.

You will come through. Always.

Focus on that mission.

# Stages of Healing From An Abusive Relationship

How do you move on from an abusive relationship?

In most cases, you do so slowly, blindly, and with immense difficulty. *Because you don't know how to.*

More likely than not, there is no *"clean break"* from the relationship. Instead, there is a long agony as you fall back into the relationship one last time *(or many)*, in your desperate desire to make it work. Peeling your heart away from your abusive partner is like prising your fingers away from a life raft.

Or at least that is how it feels at the time.

When I started my recovery, the only *"reliable"* information I had was that it would take **two years** before I would feel better.

Rest assured that that *"received wisdom"* is completely and utterly **wrong**. It is also outrageous—insamuch as it suggests that you are powerless to speed up a return to closure and happiness.

In reality, there are many powerful things that you can do to shorten the timescale and ease the pain of healing. Hence my passion for sharing with as many women as possible every last resource and revelation I discover.

Please know that every small step you take away from that old abused mindset will empower you, lift your spirits and start to restore faith in your own worth. Plus, everything that serves to demystify the process of healing will restore your confidence in your ability to heal.

Most recently, I have been thinking about **the stages of healing**. Be aware that they follow no particular timescale, and some of them may well overlap. Expect to regress from time to time at each step along the way. That is normal, even predictable. It is also unimportant as regards the final outcome. Setbacks are simply pauses that occur as you travel through the various stages. Each stage will take you further on your journey back to health and wholeness.

**The first stage of healing** starts when you finally admit that the relationship can never be what you would like it to be. This is when you acknowledge that, however much *more* you do, it will never make the relationship right.

**The second stage of healing** begins when you start to see your abusive partner as he is. You stop looking at his *"Mr Wonderful potential."* You stop explaining away his bad behaviors. Instead, you start to acknowledge the behaviors and attitudes of his that make the relationship unworkable. In short, this is the time when you **stop blaming yourself for everything**.

*(Still, you will probably continue blaming yourself for all sorts of things for a while yet… because self-blame won't disappear from your inner world overnight. It's an old habit; it dies hard.)*

**The third stage of healing** has you looking at all men as potential abusers. There may be *"helpful people,"* even sincerely caring people who will tell you that this is *"awful"* and *"wrong."* They may mean well. Good for them. Ignore them—because they cannot know the way in which you need to heal.

This third stage is immensely useful. You have finally acknowledged to yourself that **you are still at risk**—as you undoubtedly are—and you are protecting yourself. Yes, you are doing so in a very broad-brush way. But that is only right and natural. You can only start from where you are, in the best way you can, with the knowledge that you have.

Given your past experiences, would you rather be wrong and safe, or wrong and in another abusive relationship? When you are vulnerable, and—*not yet*—terribly good at seeing them coming, that is when abusers will come out of the woodwork in droves.

Don't want to believe me? Unfortunately it's all too true. You don't even have to go out looking, for abusers to find you. They'll fetch up at your home to repair the washing machine, or put down a carpet. They'll find you in the supermarket by the vegetable bins. When you are at your most vulnerable, potential abusers will assuredly find you. So a blanket belief that all men are abusers, *until proven otherwise*, is a useful belief. At this point in time, expect to encounter a lot of abusive men. Prove me wrong!

**The fourth stage of healing** comes when you start to be clear about what you want for yourself. That may be professional and/or personal. You may suddenly realize that you have made the shift from wanting above all else to share your life with *that* man, to feeling that it would be a big sacrifice to share your own precious space. Now you are starting to **put yourself at the center of your world**.

**The fifth stage of healing** comes when you start to register that there are nice men out there as well as the abusers. You may not be at all attracted to them, but you begin to notice that some of the men that you come

163

across in some contexts are gentle, considerate, respectful, fun... You fill in the rest of the qualities that matter to you.

Your antennae remain acutely sensitive, and you start to feel that you might be able to tell the difference between the two groups.

**The sixth stage of healing** comes when you feel that you can trust yourself and your judgment. You discover that the old beliefs and fears no longer have the power they once had over you.

**The more you can trust yourself, the more you can trust the world.**

This is the stage at which you are **"good to go."** Your self-doubt has fallen away.

You've learned the lessons and you can relate increasingly positively to yourself and your world.

Does this sound like fantasy right now?

Let me assure you that it is not. It is actually very doable. If I can do it—and I think I once qualified as The Most Negative Woman in Britain—so can you.

Only **commit to your recovery**, make use of the resources that are out there for you and *allow yourself* to be at whatever stage of healing you are at. Nothing that you need to do in order to promote your healing need take up much of your time—or effort. But provided you concentrate on *"allowing"* and *"observing"* yourself to travel through the healing states at your own pace, you will soon start to see change.

If an ex-Most Negative Woman In Britain says so, it has to be true.

# What the Feeling of Intense Loss is REALLY About

Much of my work is done with women who felt drawn back into relationships with their abusive partners as a result of their feelings of agonizing loneliness.

Recently, one of them stopped herself halfway through talking about her intense loneliness to admit, *"Of course, it's pretty lonely even when I am in the relationship and he treats me badly."*

Nevertheless, emotionally abusive relationships offer moments of illusory intimacy and, above all, the hope of oneness in which all your pain will fade away.

That is why so many abused women return to their nightmare relationship. They are running away from themselves. However awful the relationship is, it is, at the very least, a distraction.

From what?

Ultimately, the gaping chasm where a *positive* sense of self should be.

Of course, you could argue that what you have—as a consequence of an abusive relationship— is a negative sense of self. Until recently I would have agreed with that.

It certainly *feels* as if you have a sense of your own identity. It just happens to be a rather negative identity. But take a moment to think about it: how many times do you describe yourself in terms of what you are not? NOT confident, NOT clever, NOT outgoing, NOT slim, NOT beautiful, NOT *perfect...*

I don't know what your specific list of negatives comprises. But one thing I do know and would be prepared to put money on: you sell yourself ridiculously short. Abusive people in your life have visited their vindictive opinions on you and you have labeled yourself accordingly.

The catalogue of faults that you have been fed, and swallowed, has more or less flushed away your positive sense of self.

Because, in the end, **a sense of self can only be positive**.

But the label/identity you have swallowed is that of *"**not good enough.**"* As I write this, the coach in me bestirs herself to ask:

*"What, or more precisely **who**, are you not good enough for?"*

The answer is, obviously, that you are not good enough for your abusive partner. But here's the thing: you are never going to be good enough for Mr Nasty. In your heart of hearts, you already knew that. Didn't you?

Of course, **one day you will ask yourself in all seriousness, *"Is this man really good enough for me?"*** And on that day the answer will come back loud and clear: *"No, he is not. That man is not in my league,"* and you will finally heed it.

Until then, and even beyond that point, all sorts of old, unproductive patterns will play out in your thinking. There is one in particular that I feel I am only now beginning to make sense of, and that is the *"fallback"* position of dwelling on your perceived shortcomings. For the longest time I used to believe that that was simply an expression of self-loathing. Now, I begin to see it differently: I see it as a curious attempt to get as near to self-love as the abused mindset will let you to get.

How do I work that one out?

In terms of your heart, love is the only possible currency. Sure, there can be an absence of love *(just as there can be the absence of a positive sense of self)* and there can be the perversion of love. But still, **the only currency is love.**

**The perversion of love is, essentially, what happens in an abusive relationship.** *(That is* **perversion** *in the dictionary sense of something that is turned aside from its proper use or nature.)* Yet it is the nearest thing to *(interpersonal)* love that you are going to get in that relationship. So you clutch at it desperately, and hope you can find a magic wand to wave.

By the same token, that self-loathing, that focusing on your faults and failures has become the nearest thing to self-love that you can experience, as an abused woman. It is, I now believe, a misguided but sincere attempt to love yourself. Even as you recite to yourself those hurtful distortions, you try to find some crumbs of comfort in the place of misery in which you find yourself.

Needless to say, that doesn't work very well. But let us focus for a moment on the strategy. The strategy is to provide the nearest approximation to love and comfort that you can, when you have placed the sole source of love and comfort outside yourself, in the shape of your abusive partner.

Small wonder then, that when he, or another, *"Man"* figure, falls out of your life, you succumb instantly to that terrible sense of loss. That occurs because you don't believe that you can provide a positive expression of love for yourself. And yet you are not far short of being able to do so.

You see, the desire is ever present, the strategy already exists—only the focus is wrong.

Admittedly, bringing the focus back onto yourself is frightening. It will remain frightening for as long as you tell yourself that you are hopeless, helpless, and incapable of surviving without a man to support you. *(Not that Mr Nasty ever did much of that, when you think about it. But, hey, we are all entitled to our fantasies, however improbable they are.)*

So, **how do you learn to love yourself and be with yourself in a positive way?** As ever, one tiny step at a time. You make a point of doing **daily** small things that make you feel good. You shake yourself out of it each time you find yourself slipping into the dark well of regret and misery.

Easier said than done?

Sorry to dispel that myth, but it is surprisingly simple, if not always *easy*. A brisk walk will lift your mood; the only hard part is getting yourself outside and started.

Watching a movie tends to take you into a trance that takes you right out of yourself. Music can do the same. So can dancing. So, too, can speaking to a trusted friend who makes you laugh.

There are other things, also, that you *know* can lift your mood. Do them and you **will** feel better. Sit and ponder your loss and you **will** feel lousy.

I don't know whether you will do this or not. But I do know this: you have the choice as to whether or not to let yourself slide into that agonizing place of loss, or whether you react.

**That loss is only as real as you choose to make it.**

**The quickest things to change are your feelings.** Or they can be the slowest thing. It's all down to you and your choices.

You won't always succeed. You will fall off that wagon—probably quite a lot at the start. But I am guessing that you had the experience of falling, quite a lot, when you started learning to walk—and look how well that turned out  If you could take those falls in your stride back then, you can do so now.  Especially since every success will help you fast-track your healing.

A wise person once said to me, *"We can always do the thing we say we can't."* He was absolutely right. Women say to me all the time that they cannot change their feelings about an abusive partner, the abusive relationship, and themselves. And then they go ahead and do exactly that. You can, too.

# When It *Is* About You

Once upon a time there was a beautiful, gifted, generous young woman. She was modest also, so she didn't really believe that she could possibly be all those things. Still, she got on with her life the best way that she could.

Like all princesses, even princesses who travel through the world incognito, fairies had been present when she lay as a newborn baby in her crib.

Her fairy godmothers had done what they could to shower her with blessings.

Sadly, the wicked fairy *(or wicked witch, if you prefer)* had appeared and waved her magic wand, casting a spell that would make the baby girl susceptible to self-doubt and self-loathing.

One fairy godmother had used her last spell to bestow upon the child the gift of **intuition**—that small, quiet voice that would warn her of danger at every turn in the road.

Provided she only listened...

Somewhere along the line, the princess met a dead ringer for The Beast (as in *Beauty and the Beast*). She knew, from the moment her eyes first fell on this Beast that this creature could be very, very damaging for her.

That still, small voice warned her.

But the Beast was a cunning suitor, and he spoke long and loud.

She let his voice drown out her intuition. She became ensnared in the web of weasel words he spun.

The Princess fell for his words, of course. That was part of her job description. Just as it was part of your job description and mine...

Had her fairy godmother been able to warn her in advance of the months and years of misery she would endure as a consequence of listening to the Beast's words, maybe, just maybe, she would have walked away...

*But would* **you** *have walked away?* **Could** *you have walked away?*

This week I was talking to a woman who has reconnected with her abusive partner two years after she ended the relationship.

Now, this woman did not look back on her ex-partner with any fondness. She had done a lot of work on her recovery. She had come a long way.

But circumstances conspired to have her spend more time than she would have cared to in his company, and the old hooks started biting into her flesh once again.

Why?

Before I answer the *why*, let me tell you what actually occurred. She spent time with him, and he was at his most winsome. Some of the time at least, he was all the things that she had ever wished he could have been.

A lot of the time he was not… but she managed to overlook that. *(Funny how we do that, isn't it?)* She saw, she heard, she registered those behaviors that had always troubled her—those behaviors that, in time, would surely, once again, cause her endless pain.

Yet she could disregard those behaviors.

She simply did not feel their impact.

Why not?

*Why do we do that?*

I could offer you a really clever explanation, and I am not at all sure it would be the right one.

Yes, **abusive men are crazy-makers** and they lull you into a kind of trance; they suck you into their highly skewed worldview. That is true enough, but I don't think that that alone is a complete explanation.

Human beings have a habit, which can be both good and bad, of generalizing: just give us a fact and we will draw a generalization from it. We go from the detail to our own internal big picture *(or dream)*. And once we get invested in our own big picture, it can take wild horses to drag us back from there.

How does it work?

**We each have our own dreams**. They probably started in childhood, as a way of compensating for things that we lacked. If we felt alone in childhood, we may develop the yearning for a perfect love, for someone who will always be there for us, through thick and thin… That dream is the big picture we are—often hopelessly—drawn towards.

**We silence the voice of intuition** because we are heavily invested in that big picture, or dream.

Having silenced our fairy godmother's gift, we start the process of endowing the Beast, who has thrust himself into our consciousness, with various qualities and characteristics from our dream. We do so without thinking whether or not these qualities and characteristics are a fit with reality.

That's the joy of dreams, after all: that we can tweak things however we choose. Sadly, reality proves to be a very different affair. Try as we may, we can never tweak or mold our partner into our ideal.

Still, we give it our best shot. So his aggressiveness becomes strength, talking *(endlessly)* about his own baggage becomes sensitivity, and his neediness gets interpreted as a statement that he will cater to our needs.

How we invest in that dream!

And, because it is our dream and our generalization, it shuts out other possibilities.

Don't believe me?

Well, think about this: Have you only ever been attracted to one kind of looks in a man? Have you only ever fallen for tall, dark, and handsome? Or has your idea of what is attractive in a man changed to match the appearance of the man who currently had your heart?

Nor is it just our physical criteria that we adjust. We revise our psychological perspective also: we tell ourselves that our love object's qualities are… well, lovable. *Even when we* **know**, *beyond all doubt, that they are not.*

When the woman I mentioned earlier fell back into her old dreams about her ex-partner, she was falling into the trap of confusing her dream with the world; confusing her stale, old dream with the sum of life's possibilities.

So, it was about her, not him. It was about her feelings of scarcity. What she was *really* saying to herself, and therefore living out, was this:

*"I'm on the relationship breadline and I always will be."*

There is no better way of guaranteeing that you are, and always will be, on the relationship breadline than holding a belief like that.

Because you have gone into *"Poor me!"* thinking.

That is **not** useful.

*"Poor me!"* might be right—if your entire life was over and it had been utterly empty.

But your life is **not** over. And it does **not** have to be empty. You can still fill it with joy and meaning.

How about starting to create a new and rewarding dream?

How about starting right now?

# Why Working At Your Relationship Doesn't Work

Have you worked hard at your relationship?

It is my bet that you have.

If you are anything like most abused women, you have worked your socks off to make your relationship work. In fact, it's part of your job description: abused women are people who toil tirelessly to keep a toxic relationship alive.

You couldn't possibly pay someone enough to put in the time and the trouble that abused women sacrifice, for absolutely nothing.

Unfortunately, all of that time and trouble will never pay dividends, of course. For one simple reason:

**An abusive relationship is a relationship that is dead in the water.**

Still, from time to time, the abusive partner will give a kind of *"dead cat bounce."* Momentarily, he will show signs of the appeal he showed in the early days. This is enough for the abused partner to delude herself that, with enough intensive care from her, the relationship can be resuscitated.

It won't happen. The damage is irreversible.

But try telling that to an abused woman.

We have all heard the phrase, *"You have to work at your relationship,"* and we followed it hook, line and sinker.

I eventually realized that this is a statement that has no merit, made by moderately unhappy people to others less fortunate than themselves.

What makes me so certain?

Think about it for a moment! **Nobody works harder at relationships than an abused woman.** And the more she works at it, the worse the relationship gets.

Why?

Well, obviously the harder she works at her relationship, the less accountable her partner feels for his behaviors. If she is happy to shoulder the load, do you think that he is going to stop her? Hardly.

More importantly, *"work"* is a substitute—actually a very poor substitute—for thought. If you only stopped to *think* long enough to see the big picture, you would soon find a better outlet for your energy.

It's a little like being a miner working down a very deep mine. You don't find what you are digging for, so what do you do? You keep digging, more and more manically. And still you find nothing. If, quite literally, you came up for air and talked to other people, you might discover that the seam had long since been exhausted.

**"Working" at a relationship is a guarantee of nothing but your effort**. Nobody ever promised that your work would be requited. But somehow, inside your own head, you came to believe that if you put 10,000 or 20,000 or even 50,000 hours of *"hard work"* into your relationship, it would finally pay dividends.

Your abusive relationship is the ultimate proof that it does not. Quite the reverse: too much hard work on the part of one partner allows a bad relationship to become even worse.

So, am I saying that it is wrong to *work* at relationships?

182

Absolutely!

In fact, it is the **very worst thing an abused woman can possibly do**.

Work is not necessarily the same as committing to your relationship, investing in your relationship, and nurturing your relationship.

But here's the thing: you can only do that *if you are in a relationship*. If your *"partner"* is not prepared to commit, nurture and invest **consistently** in the relationship, then **you don't have a relationship**.

If he plays the *"breakup game"* on a regular basis, launches regular attacks on your self-worth, and trashes the *"relationship,"* then **you don't have a relationship**.

All you have is a threadbare fantasy.

One partner—*you*—*"working at it"* won't change that.

If you would only invest *in yourself* the energy and persistence you squander on a moribund relationship, and a decidedly unworthy object, have you any idea of what you could achieve, *for yourself?*

But don't take my word for it. Dare to try it for yourself. You will be amazed.

# The Opposite of Love Is Not Hate

When I asked my husband to leave and went into group counseling for abused women, one of the things that most struck me was the counselor's observation that, *"The opposite of love is not hate; it's indifference."* At the time that was a revelation to me.

The point is that **hate is simply the reverse side of the coin to love**. You cannot hate someone unless you have very strong feelings about them. When you are consumed with hurt and rage, hatred may feel like a more constructive outlet than love.

Maybe it is, maybe it isn't. Sometimes it is helpful, in the short term, to vocalize all the things you heartily disliked about your partner. The downside is, of course, that you remain just as focused, even fixated, on Mr Nasty as you were before. You are still hooked into powerful emotions that keep you locked into the relationship.

And let's not kid ourselves here. **The relationship doesn't end when Mr Nasty walks out of the door.** *(If only!)*

I was friendly for years with a woman who had stopped living with her abusive partner years ago. Their only contact occurred weekly, or fortnightly, over their two young children, and yet the abusive relationship continued to be played out as powerfully as it ever had been. They were still locked into the cycle—he of exerting power and control over her, she of trying to get her voice heard. The children were leverage for him, a hot button for her.

They were still stuck in the push-pull relationship of love and hate.

Indifference wasn't even on the horizon for those two, any more than it is for many women who are constantly breaking up with and then getting back with their ex.

So how, you might ask, do you arrive at indifference? I remember thinking that I might as well trot off in hot pursuit of the Holy Grail as aspire to indifference. Still, I flagged it up as a yardstick by which to measure my emotional involvement with my Mr Nasty.

Have I achieved indifference? I realize that this is the first time that I have asked myself that question and thought carefully about the answer.

The more time goes on, the less convinced I am that indifference is the full answer. First, nobody tells you how to arrive at indifference—and how can you possibly arrive somewhere without some kind of route map? Second, abused women are so used to being swept along on a rollercoaster of emotions that indifference is almost unimaginable. You have an emotional chasm—how will indifference fill it?

Third, the concept of indifference doesn't even *begin* to acknowledge all the emotions that you feel: the love, the hurt, the sadness, the fear, the worthlessness. I won't go on because you can name those emotions at least as well as I can.

Working with women who *know* they have to put an abusive relationship behind them, I am always struck by the problem they have with the love they still feel. They love the investment they made in the relationship; they love the person they believed their partner could be and was at bottom. The shorthand they use for this is that they loved *him*.

In a lot of cases, their supportive, caring friends and family will tell them what a jerk that partner was. He doubtless was, but that is only of limited helpfulness to the grieving woman. It may even compound her problems by making her feel like the fool he has convinced her she is.

The thing is, this woman is entitled to love her abusive partner. She is entitled to carry on loving him for the rest of her days, if she so chooses. Love after all is a choice we make. It's actually okay to carry on loving an abusive partner, if you choose. That does not mean you should ever spend time with him again and expose yourself to the destruction that he wreaks.

But **you are free to love him**.

You are also free to send him loving, healing thoughts. Since you love him, you are free to wish for his healing, as well as your own. You don't need to know what form that healing will take; you can simply wish that he finds his path so that he can grow fully into the qualities that you found lovable in him in the first instance.

Not that the two of you will *ever* get back together. You were never made for each other, in the first place. You both have your own—separate healing—to do. Part of that healing entails becoming whole, *separate* human beings.

In the best Hollywood tradition, you two poor, wounded soldiers would support each other along the same healing journey. Two hours later, you would both be whole, loving, and just about to trot off into the sunset together to the accompaniment of a great soundtrack… You would be united as never before.

In the real world none of that will happen. Your healing will take somewhat longer—but the journey will actually take you much further along the path of self-discovery and happiness. There won't just be one soundtrack, one person, one sunset. You will meet far more people along the way; you will discover so much about yourself and them. Your vistas will widen. The journey will take longer, engage more of your emotional resources and, ultimately, be a far richer experience.

And what about indifference? Will you have indifference for your abusive ex?

In the best of all possible worlds, I suspect you will not. Instead, you will have something better: detachment. You may be saddened that he does not fulfill his potential to be a loving, lovable person. But you will not be sad for *your* loss, because you will see that it is not a loss but a true gain.

By allowing yourself to acknowledge the love you feel, you set yourself free. You also set the other person free. Loving them, if that is what you choose to do, means that there is no need to own or hold on to them.

# Are You Waiting To Be Invited?

I wrote of a woman who, like so many abused women, settles for crumbs from the banquet of life. I stated that she does this because she does not really believe that there is a banquet out there.

Another reader e-mailed me to disagree with my viewpoint. I was, she felt, too harsh in my judgments. She had reached the stage *(still way short of rock bottom)* of accepting that she was a miserable person to be around. Hence, *her* Mr Nasty could not be blamed for expressing his distaste for her. In other words, the process of emotional pulverization was so far advanced that she had lost sight of all that **he** had said and done to reduce her to that state.

I can remember feeling like that also, and challenging the few people who were concerned enough to tell me my relationship was toxic. *(It undoubtedly was.)* But I had to believe in something.

When you can't believe in yourself, you end up clutching at the nearest thing that looks halfway solid. That thing is most usually your abusive partner.

My reader ended her e-mail with these words:

*"I believe there is a banquet out there, but possibly I am not invited to it due to social ineptitude or something."*

It is a statement that sounds *almost* reasonable until you *"deconstruct"* it. What saddened me *first* was the *"victim speak,"* the conviction that she was naturally and *inevitably* excluded from one of life's great blessings.

*"Victim speak"* is, of course, born of *"victim think"* and, like my reader, I too have been there and spent far, far too long there.

That doesn't make it true.

**Abused women wait to be invited to the banquet of life** when that invitation may never come. Certainly it will never come soon enough.

Then it struck me: abused women wait to be invited but the fact is that *it is not that kind of banquet.* The banquet of life is actually a self-service banquet. Anybody and everybody has an equal right to pitch up and serve themselves. They also have the same right as anyone else to sit wherever they choose and share conversation and enjoyment with whomsoever they choose.

Do they habitually exercise that equal right?

No, they do not. Instead, they focus desperately on being invited by the one person who, of all people, has an interest in excluding them from that banquet. And so they stand with their back turned to that banquet, transfixed by their abuser who, despite protestations to the contrary, does not *"do"* banquets.

Small wonder that they register no invitation.

Were they facing towards the banquet, and the people at the banquet, it is possible that some of the diners would try to include them.

Still, that is not the point.

The point is that everyone has an equal right to invite *themselves*.

Either we avail ourselves of that right or we do not. The more we avail ourselves of that right, the easier and more consistent our inclusion and welcome will be.

The reality is that the other people at the banquet naturally expect us to invite ourselves, *as they have done*. They wonder that we do not. They mistakenly assume that if we exclude ourselves it is because we do not want to be part of it, and do not want to associate with them. They will respect what they wrongly believe to be our preference.

You cannot expect other people to know more about you than you give them to understand.

Besides, it is not about them. It is all about you.

**The banquet is there**. The place is **always** there for you. It is down to you when you invite yourself. Before, I'm guessing that you didn't know how it worked. Now you do.

Invite yourself, already. Dare to claim your rightful place—the place that only you can fill.

# Freedom Is...

In recent times, there has been much talk in the UK press about a wonder drug that can, perhaps, erase traumatic memories.

How great would it be if we could erase the traumatic memories of an abusive relationship?

My own belief is that it would not be great at all; rather, it would be absolutely disastrous.

Why?

Those of us who ended up in an abusive relationship did so through our ignorance. We did not have the information, programming, wisdom—call it what you will—to see an abusive man coming. We did not have the wisdom to heed our intuition, although it doubtless tried to warn us.

If you could simply wipe out the memories, you could well end up repeating that error. You would, inevitably, be attracted once again by someone essentially very similar. The odds are high that you would repeat the same experience all over again. *(A lot of women do that anyway.)*

It is only by reviewing your *(bitter)* experience and gleaning the lessons from it that you learn:

a) not to make the same mistakes again,
b) to truly appreciate having more functional people and relationships in your life.

Plus, it is by learning the lessons of your experience that you do your part in breaking the cycle of abuse once and for all. By sharing your—admittedly hard-earned—knowledge with children, friends, and the wider world, you may be able to protect them from suffering as long and as much as you have suffered.

Further, your recovery helps speed their recovery.

Obviously, I would not presume to speak for the survivors of truly cataclysmic events. Only they have the right to say whether they would rather the horrors of their past be erased.

But for those of us whose suffering has been of the kind that is, thankfully, **un**-newsworthy, the sense that we make of that suffering can either keep us in chains or set us free. The responsibility and the choice are ours.

According to Jean-Paul Sartre, **"Freedom is what you do with what's been done to you."** Tiresome as I often find Sartre's pronouncements, I have to agree with him on that one. You free yourself from the ill treatment that has been visited on you by the way in which you process your experience.

Every week women write to me to ask, *"How could he treat me so badly?"*

The short answer is that he—that is *Mr Nasty*—did so because he had a pretty shrewd idea that he could get away with it. And he always knew how to win you round again when necessary.

He did it because he had a totally different agenda to you: you wanted to be loved; he wanted to exercise power and control over you. The more ruthless agenda won every time.

Mr Nasty will, doubtless, continue down the same track of treating you *(or your replacement)* badly for as long as he feels there is something to be gained. That being the case, continually posing the same question and looking for a different answer becomes worse than pointless. It becomes self-destructive, and totally irrelevant.

The only questions of value have to be, *"How do I move on from here?"* and *"What steps do I need to take to move into a more positive frame of mind and heal?"*

Freedom lies in what you do with your feelings of hurt.

The question, *"How could he treat me so badly?"* disempowers you.

Ask yourself instead, **"How much longer am I prepared to treat myself that badly? Why am I prepared to treat myself that badly?"**

Ask yourself also, **"How can I start to treat myself better?"** and commit to finding answers. I'm not suggesting it will be easy or obvious at the start, but it will be amazingly worthwhile.

If you do not feel you can do that alone, then work with someone who can systematically teach you how.

Freedom from the trauma of your abusive past lies in what you choose to do with what has been done to you.

What will *you* choose and **when** will you make that choice?

# How Much Faith Do You Carry Deep Within?

This morning, I awoke in a *"dark place of the soul."* As an abuse survivor, my dark places of the soul are often very dark indeed. This week there has been a *"blast from the past"* calculated to cause huge distress, a blast crafted meticulously over a period of years with a view to mortally wounding me...

Even as I write this, I can almost sense the profound empathy, tinged with curiosity, percolating through the ether, an almost involuntary wave of agreement from my readers that Life in the Abusive Kingdom is relentlessly tough.

And so it was for a good 50 minutes...

I could see exactly where I was headed... Straight into the abyss. You know the one. It's like a circle of Dante's Inferno, the one reserved for abused women. This circle is a vast, cold, barren space, filled with the sounds of wordless laments. Through the darkness you—*I*—can

197

dimly make out other eyes, other mouths, but you feel totally and utterly alone…

Desperate times call for desperate measures. Maybe thanks to the angels that watch over me—*or, at least, so I choose to believe*—I bought Dave Pelzer's book *Moving Forward*, just before this storm broke.

Now, you simply cannot quibble with Dave Pelzer; if he can rise above his horrendous early life (described in *A Child Called "It"*) there are no excuses for anyone. Certainly there are no excuses for me. A few pages in, I came across these words:

**"Never forget, your esteem is what makes you who you are. For you have been and always will be the total sum of the faith that you carry deep within!"**

Quite!

Who was I for those 50 minutes?

I was that nasty, pathetic excuse for a woman that my abusive partner had told me I was. I was the quivering personification of Mr Nasty's faith that I would never be, do or have anything, the embodiment of his loathing of women in general and me in particular. I was, in short, his construct, the sorry creature he created, and berated, in order to feel halfway good about himself.

Does that sound familiar?

**Mr Nasty's lack of esteem made me who I was**…
More correctly, *I allowed* his lack of esteem to debase
me so that I became his vision of me.

And here I was again at the same old crossroads…

Except that this time, I choose to take a different
direction.

The reality of my life is no different to the way it was
during those 50 minutes. There are upsides and
downsides; it is only my assessment of the value of that
life that counts. For 50 minutes, it was almost terminally
bleak.

And that is not how I choose to live my life now.

Elsewhere, Pelzer writes:

*"Many of those who have realized great accomplishments and awe-
inspiring achievements began with the bare, hair-thin-thread belief
that maybe, just maybe, things might get better."*

Every one of us has those hair-thin-thread beliefs. Sure,
an abuser will do what he can to rubbish them; but try as
he may, he cannot *ever* sever them. Those hair-thin
threads cannot be cut.

Thank you, Dave, for reminding me of those hair-thin-thread beliefs! Thin they may be, but they are strong enough to carry your weight if you will only let them, for as long as you let them. The one thing that you have to do is trust them when you can, as much as you can.

Only you know what your hair-thin-thread belief is. Your abusive partner may have ridiculed it, you may have overlooked it for the longest time, *and yet* it is still there. It is part of your God-given programming, hardwired into your being.

However desperate your circumstances may look, that hair-thin-thread belief remains. If it worked for Dave Pelzer, how could it not work for you?

# How Do You Want To Be Loved?

**All abusive relationships start with compromise.**

My experience of listening to the stories of hundreds and hundreds of abused women suggests three levels of compromise:

- Dislike at first sight. I have yet to come across one abused woman whose initial, *instantaneous* reaction to her future partner was not a resounding, *"Yuck!"*
- Accepting and overlooking distasteful and/or troubling behaviors—including leering at other women, emotional bullying, threats, addictions, etc.
- Settling for less.

Now, the notion of *settling for less* needs some expansion. There is a notion that, especially if you have reached 30 or so, your *"biological clock is ticking"* and you should be prepared to settle for Mr Good Enough.

I don't buy that one—at all. As you know to your cost, it is a dangerous notion indeed. Abused women are pitifully **bad** at identifying Mr Good Enough, or even Mr Halfway Good, correctly.

Too many women end up in abusive relationships because their internal dialogue goes something like this:

*"Well, you might as well face it; you're not so hot. You can't expect anyone really fabulous to come along, so you might as well make do with this guy. He's the best you can hope for. Especially as being with him gives you an opportunity to stand in his shadow and hide your inadequacies behind him."*

The bottom line for women who end up in an abusive relationship is that they don't know how they want to be loved.

They don't know how they want to be loved because they had no experience in their formative years of being truly loved and accepted *unconditionally*.

*They had no experience of being good enough, just as they were, just because...*

A person would be more inclined to put up with an abusive, critical partner, would they not, if experience had taught them that they never had been and were never going to be *"good enough"*?

202

**Part of the healing process for abused women is learning to love themselves.**

When you think about it—which you probably don't very much—loving yourself costs nothing, and harms nobody.

When you are constantly striving to give love without receiving love, you are running on empty—and that, inevitably, harms you. When you can love yourself, giving and receiving love becomes much, much easier, because your love tank is always being replenished.

Still, making the shift from the self-loathing that has been programmed into you by Mr Nasty to self-love is not easy. This is why it is so important for abused women to start to focus on the good feelings they get from other people, rather than on the bad feelings an abusive partner arouses in them.

Some women who leave an abusive relationship are in a rush to dive into the next relationship. Others don't even want to contemplate another relationship ever again.

I've no doubt that taking the time to be relationship-free, long enough to heal and learn to truly love themselves, is the best thing that abused women can possibly do.

But still, it is really useful to ask yourself, *"How do I want to be loved?"*

*Especially* if you don't have any clear answer.

Envisioning how you want to be loved will help you to discover what is valuable and lovable about you. In order to have a vision of how you want to be loved, you **have to** enter into a more loving dialogue with yourself. You have to move from the habitual self-loathing dialogue to a more constructive way of relating to yourself.

So here's a clue: how you want to be loved is actually the way that you want to be treated. That is something you need to be very, very specific about. Settling for less is extremely dangerous; you've already tried it, so you know how much it has cost you.

The way you want to be treated is **not** about your financial circumstances; it's not about being showered with expensive gifts, or any of the public trappings of a relationship. What it *is* about is the dynamics of your relationship.

If you want to feel loved, what specific behaviors will show you that you are loved?

If you want to feel respected, how will your partner's behavior *towards you* show you that you are respected?

If you want to feel valued, what will your partner have to say, and do, to show you that you are valued?

If you want to feel treated as an equal, how will you know that he does treat you as an equal?

If you want to feel cherished, how will your partner's behavior show you that you are cherished?

How good will it feel to have someone in your life who really, really cares about your feelings?

Good, huh?

So now for the killer question:

*Why would you imagine that anybody else is going to do for you what you are not prepared to do for yourself?*

Every small step you take towards loving yourself brings that feeling of being loved and lovable that much closer.

Neither you nor I can know if or when you will have another partner in your life. Right now, that doesn't even matter.

But you can start feeling loved and lovable right now. Plenty of people in your life will be willing to reflect that message back to you, just as soon as you start to feel it for yourself.

Even if you can only feel it for yourself for 30 seconds at a time, that is a useful start.

Try it, and you will see.

# What Seeds Have You Planted Beneath The Snow?

A while back, soon after I first dipped my toe back into the dating pool, I took a BIG risk and did something I had not done before in the *"real world"*: I shared the truth with a man about my abusive marriage.

Well, I say *"shared,"* and that is what I intended. It ended up being rather more of a *"dump."* Maybe I should specify that I didn't share the whole 20-plus years in glorious Technicolor, but I did divulge my truth about those years. *(It took about 15-20 minutes.)*

And the lesson I learned from it? The lesson was, undoubtedly, that you really don't want to visit too much information on a man too soon if you want him to stick around.

*(From that point of view, it was a fascinating process. It seems to work like this: Give a man a couple of pieces of information he*

*finds hard to process and he will rapidly stop listening to you.*
*Instead he creates his own narrative, which may well be very far*
*removed from anything you happen to be saying or attempting to*
*convey.)*

So what was my purpose in doing that?

My purpose to put my truth out there. I overshared so
spectacularly because I had become aware that the fear
and shame that grew out of my abusive relationship were
still *"drivers"* in my life. I wanted to clear them.

Somehow I knew that, in order to clear them, there were
things that I needed to say out loud. I needed to hear
myself say them and, ultimately, bounce them off a man.
Had he been able to truly hear me, that would have been
splendid. And surprising.

As it turned out, he couldn't and it really didn't matter.
Because **I heard me**.

He didn't hear the courage and he certainly didn't get the
point of what I was doing. He couldn't understand why
feeling emotionally safe was vitally important to me. Nor
did he understand how important it was for me to
liberate myself from the shame that had silenced my
voice for years and years.

All he could understand was that our experience of
relationships was different. *(Well, yes!)* And that I didn't

share his belief that having a relationship is as easy as falling off a log. *(And he was acting like **I** was from planet Zog!)* He certainly could not understand why I would spoil his pleasant evening with a load of ugly feelings that he could not relate to.

So why did I do it?

Having spent years thinking about relationships and working with people, particularly women, around relationships, I believe that there is a skill to creating and conducting a successful relationship. I wanted to know whether or not this man could *hear* me and respond in such a way that we might have the promise of a worthwhile future together.

Heaven knows it's easy to fall into a relationship: there is a natural feel-good factor to new relationships that can tend to last around two years—always assuming that you haven't stumbled upon an A1 abuser. But then the stardust disappears and the relationship will only work as well as you and your partner can make it work. *(Unless you are both still concussed from falling off that log.)*

So much for the theory. The man in question, being a *true man*, didn't *"do"* theory. I am happy to acknowledge that and thank him for his part in my process.

He is by no means a bad man, not out for power and control. Still, he took refuge behind the serried mythological ranks of *"most men."* *"Most men"* would not have been able to take on board what I was saying. *"Most men"* would not accept my views about relationships. *"Most men"*…

Once upon a time, that *"most men"* rhetoric would have left me feeling diminished and inadequate. But no more.

**I am not "most women" and I don't want "most men."** *"Most women"* and *"most men"* are lowest common denominators.

I have not survived all the misery of an abusive relationship just to settle for being a shadow of who I truly am, or to settle for the lowest common denominator. I don't believe that you have, either. You have done misery, humiliation, pain, and shame—and you **know** that doesn't work for you.

You may or may not be as far along your journey as to get back into dating, *yet*. But at some point you may decide that you both want a healthy, fulfilling, intimate relationship and are ready to start the process of creating one.

The stumbling block for you right now may be where you find all the resources that you need in order to trust and not make the same mistakes again. Believe me, those resources all lie within you. I can't tell you exactly where, or when, you will find them, but I know that you will. I see it in myself and I see it, again and again, in the women I work with.

For the longest time—or certainly what *feels* like the longest time—those resources are not there. And then one day they are.

How does it happen?

For me, it is all about the seeds planted beneath the snow.

Somehow, even in your darkest hours, you have been planting those seeds. You plant seeds:

- whenever you refuse to settle for second best – or worse
- whenever you take the time to read something like this
- whenever you affirm what it is you want more of in your life
- whenever you take a step forward, however tiny it is, however fearfully you take it.

The chances of seeing results fast are small. Not least because you focus more on sameness and your shortcomings than you do on difference. But you will see results. Just do what you can, when you can, from where you are, and you will **see results**. It is an inevitable part of the process of life and change. Only truly set your course, and it must take you in that direction.

And if you are committed to speeding up that process, think seriously about working with someone who, like me, understands and is committed to your healing.

# Next Steps

*You already know what I am going to say, don't you?*

If you recognize yourself and your partner in the pages of this book, you know what you need to do. You need to **get out, and stay out**.

But maybe you are still not ready to hear that.

That's okay. I can remember a time when someone said that to me—although they could not offer a truly convincing explanation of why my marriage was doomed—and I ended up hating the messenger.

That was one way to avoid focusing on the message.

So, I *"listened to my heart,"* stayed for more years, while I lost more and more of my identity and self-worth. I only dragged myself away when I knew I was drowning and if I didn't come up for air soon, I never would.

It is my sincere wish for you that you do it better than that.

If you can leave now—that is, if you are *ready to leave*— then do it. But first plan your departure very carefully.

Leaving an abusive man can be a very dangerous business. There is a greater tendency for abusive men to be violent when a partner decides to leave—or after she has left. So you will need to have a clear strategy in place to protect yourself. You can find out more about what you need to need to do through some simple internet research. *(One helpful guide can be found at http://nprdap.org/safety-planning/.)*

Above all, do not imagine you can have a civilized discussion about ending the relationship with a partner who has shown himself to be *un*civilized through the course *(curse)* of the relationship. Sadly, it won't happen.

Freeing yourself of an abusive partner is a tricky, unpleasant process. However, it remains the best alternative for you and your children.

If possible, gather information about the true state of your joint finances and assets you share with your partner *before* you leave. Too often I've heard abused women say, *"Oh, he says he will share everything 50-50."*

*Why would he?*

You haven't been an equal partner in his life until now. Why do you suppose he would suddenly behave nobly towards you?

It's not going to happen.

### And what if you can't leave yet?

Then **start putting yourself at the center of your own life**.

**Start treating yourself *like you matter*.** Start identifying some of your own wants and needs, and see if and where you can begin to get them met. Make sure you do things that you enjoy, even the simplest things, like sipping a cappuccino, or reading a good book in peace, or spending time with friends.

**Learn to say "No."** Practice with children, friends, or family members you trust. This is how you start to build boundaries for yourself.

**Start to envision the life that you want to have.** Do what you can to imagine what that life will be like, who will be in it with you, how it will *feel*. Start to revive the joyful aspects of your character which your abusive partner has stifled for so long.

**Stop taking sole responsibility for everything that goes wrong in your relationship.** There are two of you in the relationship *(allegedly)*; therefore the problems cannot all be your fault. *No matter what he says.*

**Get the support you need.** I stayed in my abusive marriage for years longer than I should have done *because I believed I had to "go it alone" and "make it work."* The women I work with have the confidence to break up with their abusive partner far, far sooner than they otherwise would have done.

I know **exactly** how scary it is to walk away from an abusive relationship. I also know how happy women are once they have done it.

*Do they ever regret their abusive partner?*

Not at all. Once they have had the help they need to understand the true nature of the relationship, they see that it was fatally doomed to failure, right from the start. They also see that they have much, **much** more going for them than they ever thought they had. That leaves them with **no regrets** whatsoever.

Oh, and they don't ever talk about still loving their abusive partner, either. *Because that love disappears with the realization of who that partner really was.* Once the Mr Wonderful construct falls away, they see him for the millstone around their neck that he always was.

*When you imagine leaving your abusive partner and it makes you sad, is it because you see a life filled with joy, laughter and love?*

*Or is it because you imagine your life without him as being even more hollow than it is now?*

Your life without an abusive partner can *only* be more fulfilling than your life with him.

On the other hand, you can only move on when the time is right for you. Either way, **keep reading and learning**.

I'd like you to think about having a Tipping Point.

Why is it that it takes some people longer to do a thing than it does others?

Because they need more input. They need to feel 100% sure about what they are going to do. That is not good, or bad. It is just the way they are made.

If you need more input and information to support you in making what will be life-changing decisions about your relationship, you will find plenty more resources on my website, *http://recoverfromemotionalabuse.com*.

Finally, I wish you all the peace, happiness, and fulfillment that **I know** lies ahead for you once you start to move along your healing journey.

If I can be part of that in any way and make your healing journey smoother, easier, and faster, I will be delighted.

Warm wishes,

*Annie*

# About Annie Kaszina

Annie spent 20 years in an abusive marriage, *"covering up"* for a wounded *(and wounding)* emotionally abusive man, and hoping against hope that she could love him into wholeness… so that, one day, he would love her into wholeness.

She became very, very good at putting her own life on hold and pursuing a doomed career as a people pleaser.

Eventually, she could take no more. She realized that she had to get out—or fall apart.

She left, and set about getting the help she needed to heal.

That process was slow and painful. She discovered a lot about abusive men and abusive relationships. But nobody could tell her how to heal the hurt, the shame, the fear, and the self-loathing.

She spent years discovering what really works. Plus, she discovered that there is a really great life after abuse.

She has made it her mission to share everything she knows, and do whatever she can to help as many other women as possible along the journey back to wholeness. She is passionate about breaking the mold of abuse, once and for all, and helping women to create great relationships.

Having *"deconstructed"* precisely how she, and other bright, loving women, end up in horrible relationships with abusive men, Annie now has a lovely partner. She has now enjoyed a decade of happiness with this gentle, sweet-natured caring man – who never creates a drama or spoils an occasion.

When not working with women around relationships, Annie loves to spend time with dear friends and her lovely partner. She also enjoys spending quality time with Basil K, her precious, footballing Shih Tzu, who occasionally contributes to Annie's coaching sessions with a well-timed bark or the squeak of a favorite toy!

If you would like to work personally with Annie, on any relationship issue, you can contact her at:

**annie@RecoverFromEmotionalAbuse.com**

# Further Resources

If **"Married to Mr Nasty"** has helped you and you would like further information and resources to guide you along the different stages of your healing journey, options include:

**"The Woman You Want To Be"\*** This book will accompany you through a year of emotional healing. It is designed to help you grow your self-esteem—even if you currently feel you have none. It is a very useful tool for working on yourself, creating the strength, self-belief, and above all trust that you need to take control of the reins of your life once more.

**"The Emotional Abuse Healing Journey"\*** This comprehensive 17-module audio program, with transcripts, will give you the information, techniques, insights, and vision you need to heal your heart, put the trauma of your abusive relationship behind you. It will also teach you how to spot an abuser in the future, before you get hurt. Every module explores, in depth, one aspect of abusive relationships.

**"Do You Choose Your Dog More Carefully Than Your Husband?"** This multi-award winning book is suitable for any woman who is thinking about getting back into the world of dating and relationships and wants to avoid further pain heartbreak. Jam-packed with insights, mind-shifting exercises and laugh-out-loud

220

moments, this book will transform the way you view yourself, your relationships, and your path to lasting love.

**Personal Coaching\*** This is my VIP coaching 1-2-1 program for women who want to work one-on-one with me, to make change happen. If you feel you need more personal support, and want a specifically tailored healing journey and the benefits of working, intensively, one-on-one with me, this is the right program for you.

\* All of these resources are available at **http://recoverfromemotionalabuse.com**.

Plus, you can opt in to receive free weekly tips, tools and information to guide your along your healing journey direct to your Inbox.

Made in the USA
Columbia, SC
29 March 2021

35232125R00133